The Saga of Thorstein the White

Original Text, Translations, and Word Lists

Translated by
Matthew Leigh Embleton

The Saga of Thorstein the White

Cover: Old Norse text over an outline of Iceland. Author's design.

Acknowledgments

I have long been fascinated by languages and history, and I am very grateful to the special people in my life who have supported and encouraged me in my work. Thank you for believing in me. You know who you are.

Introduction

Old Norse is a North Germanic language spoken by inhabitants of Scandinavia from about the 7th to the 15th centuries. Old Icelandic is a variety of Old West Norse that emerged during the Norse settlement of Iceland in the second half of the 9th century. The rich tradition of Icelandic literature survived by oral tradition over several centuries before being written down in the 13th Century. The Saga of Thorstein the White (*Þorsteins saga hvíta*) is one of the many Sags of Icelanders or *Íslendingasögur*. The word '*saga*' (plural: '*sǫgur*' or '*sögur*') translates as 'what is said', an 'utterance', an 'oral account', or a 'notification'.

This book contains:

- The Saga of Thorstein the White (*Þorsteins saga hvíta*) (Old Norse Version)
- An Old Norse to English Word List
- An English to Old Norse Word List
- The Saga of Thorstein the White (*Þorsteins saga hvíta*) (Old Icelandic Version)
- An Old Icelandic to English Word List
- An English to Old Icelandic Word List
- A Word Comparison of Old Norse and Old Icelandic words

The texts are presented in their original form, with a literal word-for-word line-by-line translation, and a Modern English translation, all side-by-side. In this way, it is possible to see and feel how the worked and how it has evolved. This book is designed to be of use and interest to anyone with a passion for the Old Norse or Old Icelandic language, Norse history, or languages and history in general.

The Saga of Thorstein the White (*Old Norse*)

Old Norse	Literal	English
1	1	1
Maðr hét Ölvir inn hvíti.	Man named Olvir the white.	There was a man named Olvir the White.
Hann var Ásvaldsson Göngu-Hrólfssonar, Öxna-Þórissonar.	He was son-of-Osvald son-of-Gongu-Hrolf, son-of-Oxna-Thori.	He was the son of Osvald, son of Gongu-Hrolf, son of Oxna-Thori.
Hann var lendr maðr í Nóregi ok bjó í Naumudal.	He was land man of Norway and lived in Naumudal.	He was a landed man of Norway and lived in Naumudal.
Hann stökk fyrir ófriði Hákonar jarls á Yrjar ok dó þar.	He fled before war Hakon earl on Yrjar and died there.	He fled before the war with earl Hakon on Yrjar and died there.
Hann átti einn son barna, er Þorsteinn hét ok var kallaðr Þorsteinn hvíti.	He had one son born, was Thorstein named and was called Thorstein white.	He had one son born who was named Thorstein and was called Thorstein the White.
Hann fór þegar eptir andlát föður síns út til Íslands með alla fjárhluti sína ok kom skipi sínu í Vápnafjörð,	He travelled straight-away after death father his out to Iceland with all possessions his and came ship his to Vopnafjord,	He travelled straight-away after the death of his father out to Iceland with all his possessions and his ship came to Vopnafjord.
en þá var lokit landnámum á öllu Íslandi.	but then was ended land-taking of all Iceland.	But then all the land taking of Iceland had ended.
Sá maðr bjó at Hofi í Vápnafirði, er hét Steinbjörn ok var kallaðr körtr, ok hafði honum þetta land gefit Eyvindr föðurbróðir hans, allt á milli Vápna ok Vestrdalsár.	The man lived at Hof in Vopnafjord, was named Steinbjorn and was called Kartur, and had he this land given Eyvind father-brother his, all in between Vopnafjord and Vesturdalsa.	There was a man living at Hof in Vopnafjord named Steinbjorn. He was called Kartur and he had been given land there by his uncle eyvind, between Vopnafjord and Vesturadalsa.
Steinbjörn var eyðslumaðr mikill í búinu.	Steinbjorn was spending-man much in estate.	Steinbjorn spent much on his estate.

Old Norse	Literal	English
En sem Þorsteinn vissi þat, at lönd váru öll numin áðr, fór hann á fund Steinbjarnar, ok kaupir hann at honum land ok reisir bú á Tóptavelli ok bjó þar nökk vetr, ok varð honum gott til fjár ok metnaðar.	But as Thorstein knew it, to lands were all taken before, travelled he to find Steinbjorn, and bought he to him land and raised farm at Toftavellir and dwelt there some winters, and became he good to wealth and ambition.	But when Thorstein knew that the lands were all taken before, he travelled to find Steinbjorn and bought land from him and raised a farm at Toftavellir, and stayed there several winters, and he became good in wealth and ambition.
Hann hafði skamma stund í búi verit, áðr hann fór ok leitaði sér ráðs ok bað konu þeirar, en Ingibjörg hét ok var dóttir Hróðgeirs ins hvíta Hrafnssonar.	He had short while at estate been, before he went and sought him advice and proposed-to woman there, but Ingibjorg named and was daughter Hrodgeir the white son-of-Hrafn.	He had been at the estate a short while when he sought the hand of a woman who was named Ingibjorg, and she was the daughter of Hrodgeir the White, son of Hrafn.
Hennar fekk hann.	Her married he.	He married her.
Við þessari konu átti hann fimm börn.	With this wife had he five children.	With this wife he had five children.
Sonr hans hét Önundr, annarr Þórðr, þriði Þorgils.	Son his named Onund, another Thord, third Thorgils.	His son was named Onund, another Thord, and the third Thorgils.
Dætr hans hétu Þorbjörg ok Þóra.	Daughters his named Thorbjorg and Thora.	His daughters were named Thorbjorg and Thora.
Þorgils var inn mannvænligsti maðr.	Thorgils was then man-most-promising man.	Thorgils was the most promising man.
Þorsteinn græddi fé í ákafa.	Thorstein profited wealth with zeal.	Thorstein built up his wealth with zeal.
Steinbirni kört varð féfátt ok fór á fund Þorsteins ok beiddist fjárláns af honum.	Steinbjorn short was money-few and went he to-meet Thorstein's and to-ask fee-loan of him.	Steinbjorn was short of money and went to meet Thorstein to ask him for a loan.
Þorsteinn er ok góðr af fjárláninu, ok þangat til tekr hann lán af Þorsteini, at harðla mjök eyðist fé Steinbirni, ok þykkir Þorsteini versna skulda-nautrinn ok þykkir óvíss skuldastaðrinn at Steinbirni.	Thorstein was and good of fee-loaning, and from-there to take him loan from Thorstein, to harden much spending wealth Steinbjorn's, and considered Thorstein worst debtor and seemed uncertain debt to Steinbjorn.	Thorstein was good to lend him money, and Steinbjorn spent this wealth so much that Thorstein considered him the worst debtor, and it seemed uncertain if Steinbjorn would repay his debt.

Old Norse	Literal	English
Ok nú heimtir hann féit, ok lýkst með því þeira fjár reiður, at Steinbjörn geldr Þorsteini Hofland, ok fór Þorsteinn byggðum til Hofs ok kaupir sér goðorð ok gerist inn mesti sveitarhöfðingi.	And now demanded he fee, and ended with therefore their finances decided, to Steinbjorn paid Thorstein Hofland, and travelled Thorstein settlements to Hof and bought himself chieftain and was then best rural-chief.	And now he demanded the money to settle their finances, and so it was that Steinbjorn paid Thorstein with the land Hof, and Thorstein travelled to Hof and bought himself a chieftaincy, and he was the best rural chief.
Hann var allra manna vinsælastr.	He was all people popular.	He was popular with all the people.
Ok er Þorsteinn hafði búit marga vetr á Hofi, þá gerðust þau tíðendi at herbergjum hans, at Ingibjörg tók sótt ok andaðist.	And when Thorstein had lived many winters on Hof, then made the tidings to rooms his, to Ingibjorg took sickness and died.	And when Thorstein had lived for many winters at Hof, then the news at his household was that Ingibjorg took sickness and died.
Þorsteini þótti þetta skaði mikill, en helt þó búi sínu sem áðr.	Thorstein thought this loss great, but held though estate his as before.	Thorstein thought this loss great, but continued to hold his estate as before.
## *2*	## 2	## 2
Maðr hét Þórir.	Man named Thori.	There was a man named Thori.
Hann var sonr Atla, sem bjó í Atlavík fyrir austan vatn.	He was son-of Atli, as lived in Atlavik before east water.	He was the son of Atli who lived in Atlavik before the east water.
Þar eru nú sauðhús.	There were now sheep-house.	There are now sheep houses there.
Þórir var kvángaðr.	Thori was married.	Thori was married.
Kona hans hét Áslaug ok var dóttir Brynjólfs ins gamla.	Wife his names Auslag and was daughter Brynolf's the old.	His wife's name was Asvor who was the daughter of Brynolf the Old.
Þau Þórir áttu tvau börn.	Then Thori had two children.	Then Thori had two children.
Hét sonr þeira Einarr, en Ásvör dóttir.	Named son theirs Einar, and Asvor daughter.	Their son was named Einar, and their daughter Asvor.
Einarr var vaskligr ok ekki stórr maðr, hávaðamaðr mikill ok í meðallagi vinsæll.	Einar was diligent and not great man, a-loud-man much and of middle-lying popularity.	Einar was diligent but not a large man, a loud man and of moderate popularity.

Old Norse	Literal	English
Ásvör var kvenna vænst ok vinsælust.	Asvor was woman fair and popular.	Asvor was a fair woman and was popular.
Þat gerðist til tíðenda á hag Þorsteins hvíta, at hann tók augnaverk svá mikinn, at þar fyrir missti hann sjónina.	That became to news that benefit Thorstein's white, to he took eye-injury so much, to there before lost his sight.	It became news that Thorstein the White had an injury in his eyes, so much that he lost his sight.
Þykkist vanfærr til umsýslu, ræðr nú um við Þorgils, biðr hann taka við liðinu.	Seemed disabled to administration, discussed now about with Thorgils, bid he take with team.	He considered himself disabled in his administration, he now discussed with Thorgils, asking him to take over.
Þorgils sagði þat skylt, at hann veitti slíkt fulltingi, er hann má.	Thorgils said that should, to he grant such assistance, as he may.	Thorgils said that it should be that he grant him any assistance that he may.
Faðir hans ræðr við hann, at hann fái sér kvánfang ok biði Ásvarar Þórisdóttur,	Father his discussed with him, to he get himself wife and asked Asvar Daughter-of-Thorri,	His father discussed with him that he should get himself a wife, and ask for the hand of Asvar, daughter of Thorri.
ok þat varð, ok fór hon með honum til búsins, ok tókust með þeim ástir góðar, ok áttu tvau börn.	and that became, and travelled she with him to farm, and took with them love good, and had two children.	And so it became, and she travelled with him to the farm and they took to loving each other well and had two children.
Sonr þeira hét Helgi, en dóttir Guðrún.	Son theirs named Helgi, and daughter Gudrun.	Their son was named Helgi, and their daughter Gudrun.
Þorgils var þá vel tuttugu vetra.	Thorgils was then well twenty winters.	Thorgils was then twenty winters old.

3

Hrani hét maðr ok var kallaðr gullhöttr.	Hrani named man and was called gold-hat.	There was a man named Hrani who was called Gold Hat.
Hann var fóstri Þorgils, en frændi konu hans.	He was fosterer Thorgils, but cousin woman his.	He was foster father to Thorgils and a cousin of Asvar's.
Hann var hávaða maðr mikill ok var heimamaðr at Hofi ok var kallaðr grályndr.	He was loud man much and was home-man to Hof and was called gralyndr.	He was very much a loud man, and was of the household at Hof, and was called malicious.
Þorkell hét maðr ok var kallaðr flettir.	Thorkell named man and was called flettir.	There was a man named Thorkell, and he was called Fleecer.

Old Norse	Literal	English
Hann var heimamaðr at Hofi ok frændi þeira Hofverja, mikill ok sterkr.	He was home-man to Hof and kinsman theirs of-Hof, great and strong.	He was a man of the household at Hof, and a kinsman of theirs, he was great and strong.
Þorbjörn hét maðr.	Thorbjorn named man.	There was a man named Thorbjorn.
Hann bjó í Sveinungsvík.	He lived in Sveinungsvik.	He lived in Sveinungsvik.
Þat er á millum Melrakkasléttu ok Þistilsfjarðar.	That was in between Melrakkasletta and Thistilsfjord.	It was inbetween Melrakkasletta and Thistilsfjord.
Þorbjörn var drengr góðr ok rammr at afli, vinr góðr Þorsteins hvíta.	Thorbjorn was fellow good and strong to force, friend good Thorstein's white.	Thorbjorn was a good fellow, and a strong man of force, and a good friend of Thorstein the White.
Maðr er nefndr Þorfinnr.	Man was named Thorfin.	There was a man named Thorfin.
Hann bjó á Skeggjastöðum í Hnefilsdal.	He lived on Skeggjastadir in Hnefilsdal.	He lived in Skeggjastadir in Hnefilsdal.
Hann átti ok enn annat bú.	He had and one other estate.	He had also another estate.
Þorgerðr hét kona hans.	Thorgerd named wife his.	His wife was named Thorgerd.
Þau áttu þrjá sonu, ok hét Þorsteinn sonr þeira ok var kallaðr fagri, annarr Einarr, þriði Þorkell.	Then had three sons, and named Thorstein son theirs and was called fair, another Einar, third Thorkell.	Then they had three sons, their son was named Thorstein who was known as the Fair, another was Einar, and the third Thorkell.
Allir váru þeir mannvænligir.	All were they men-promising.	They were all promising men.
Þorsteinn var fyrir þeim bræðrum.	Thorstein was before them brothers.	Thorstein was the leader of the brothers.
Hann var fullkominn at aldri, er hér er komit sögunni.	He was full-coming to age, as here was coming the-saga.	He was coming of age as here the story comes.
Kraki hét maðr ok bjó á bæ þeim, er heitir á Kraka læk.	Kraki named man and lived on farm that, was named on Kraki brook.	There was a man named Kraki, and he lived at a farm named Krakalaek.
Kraki var vel auðigr maðr, kvángaðr maðr, ok hét kona hans Guðrún.	Kraki was well wealthy man, married man, and named wife his Gudrun.	Kraki was a wealthy man, a married man, and his wife's name was Gudrun.

Old Norse	Literal	English
Þau áttu dóttur eina barna, er Helga hét ok var allra kvenna friðust, ok þótti sá kostr beztr í Fljótsdalsheraði.	Then had daughter one children, was Helga named and was all women most-beautiful, and seemed so choice best among Fljotsdalsheradi.	They had only one child, a daughter named Helga, and she was the most beautiful of all women, and so it seemed the best choice among the district of Fljotsdal.
Þess er getit, at Þorsteinn fagri beiddist fjárláns tillaga af föður sínum ok kvaðst vilja af landi burt.	This was told-of, to Thorstein fair asked fee-loan proposal from father his and said willed of land away.	It was told that Thorstein the Fair asked for a loan from his father, saying that he wished to travel to lands far away.
Þorfinnr kvað svá vera skyldu.	Thorfin said so be should.	Thorfin said that so it should be.
Leggr hann til slíkt, sem hann beiddist.	Laid he to such, as he asked.	He gave him such as he asked for.
Hefir hann verit í förum nökkur sumur.	Had he been about travelling some summers.	He had been travelling about for several summers,
Verðr honum gott til fjár ok metnaðar, ok hvert sinn, er hann var útan, lagði hann eptir nökkut af fjárhlut þeim, er hann þóttist þurfa ok faðir hans.	Became him good to wealth and ambition, and each that, when he was out-of, left he after some of fee-lot they, as he thought needed and father his.	He became good in wealth and ambition, and each time that he went out, he kept behind some money that he thought he and his father would need.
Ok eitt vár, er Þorsteinn var út hér um vetrinn, kemr Einarr Þórisson at máli við föður sinn ok beiddist af honum tillag ok segist vilja fara til félags við Þorstein.	And one spring, when Thorstein was back here about winter, came Einar son-of-Thorri to speak with father his and asked of him proposal and said willed travel to company with Thorstein.	And one spring when Thorstein was back here around winter, came Einar son of Thorri to speak with his father, he asked him about his proposal to travel in company with Thorstein.
Þorsteinn kvaðst eigi mundu synja Einari félags ok gefr honum skip hálft, telr þó, at honum segi í meðallagi hugr um félag þeira fyrir sakir óvin veitts skaplyndis Einars.	Thorstein said not would refuse Einar company and gave him ship half-share, counted though, to he said of middle-lying thought about company theirs before sake-of un-friend bestowing temper Einar's.	Thorstein said that he would not refuse Einar the company, and he gave him a half share of the ship. He counted himself only moderately eager about their company for the sake of Einar's unfriendly temper.
Þeir fóru útan ok lögðu félag saman.	They went out and laid company together.	They went out and had their company together.

Old Norse	Literal	English
Þorsteinn heldr öllu til virðingar Einari ok virði hann í öllu mest, ok þó lagðist svá á, at Þorsteinn var meira virðr en Einarr af öðrum mönnum fyrir þess sakir, at hann reyndist góðr drengr ok vinveittr í skaplyndi.	Thorstein held all to worthiness Einar and valued him to all most, and though lay so on, to Thorstein was more respect than Einar of other people for this sake, to he turned-out good fellow and friendly in temper.	Thorstein held Einar in worthiness, and honoured him most in all things, and so it lay that Thorstein was more respected than Einar by other people, for the sake of the fact that he was a good fellow with a friendly temper.
Fór vel um stund félag þeira.	Travelled well about awhile company theirs.	They travelled well for awhile in their company.
# 4	# 4	# 4
Þat er sagt, einn vetr, at þeir váru útan hér fóst bræðr, at Þorfinnr kemr at máli við Þorstein, hvern hann ætlaði sinn ráðahag at sumri.	That was said, one winter, to they were out here foster brothers, to Thorfin came to speak with Thorstein, what he intended that proposed to summer.	It was said that one winter, the foster brothers were out, and that Thorfin came to speak with Thorstein, about what he proposed to do that summer.
Þorsteinn kvaðst útan ætla.	Thorstein said out-of intended.	Thorstein said that he intended to be going out.
Þorfinnr kvaðst biðja vilja hann, at hann tæki við búi með honum.	Thorfin said ask willed he, to he take with estate with him.	Thorfin said that he rather wished to take over the estate with him.
Þorsteinn svaraði ok sagðist engan hug hafa á því, en kvað hann slíkt hafa af hans gózi, sem hann vildi.	Thorstein answered and said none thoughts had about for, but said he such had of his belongings, which he wished.	Thorstein answered and said that he had no thoughts about it, but that he had all the belongings that he wished.
Þorsteinn hafði mikit fé í förum.	Thorstein had much wealth to travel.	Thorstein had much wealth to travel.
Þorfinnr lézt hugsat hafa ráð fyrir honum ok lézt vilja biðja honum til handa Helgu Krakadóttur.	Thorfin let know had advice for him and let willed ask him for hand Helga's daughter-of-Kraka.	Thorfin let him know that he had advice for him, and that he wished for him to have the hand of Helga daughter of Kraka.
Þorsteinn kvað sér þat ofráð, er hon stóð ein til alls arfs eptir Kraka.	Thorstein said he that too-high, was she stood alone to all inheritance after Kraki.	Thorstein said that he found this too much, because she alone stood to inherit Kraki's estate.
Þorfinnr kvað vera jafnræði, bæði fyrir ættar sakir ok mannanar.	Thorfin said be equally, both for noble sake and accomplishment.	Thorfin said that it would be an equal match for their nobility and their prospects.

Old Norse	Literal	English
Fara þeir nú ok vekja þetta mál við Kraka.	Went they now and awoke this matter with Kraki.	They now went and raised the matter with Kraki.
Hann kallar sér þetta vel at skapi.	He calls himself this well to mood.	He said that it was well to his liking.
Var þetta mál upp borit fyrir Helgu, ok fundust eigi afsvör í hennar máli.	Was this matter up borne for Helga, and found not of-answer in her matter.	The matter was borne up with Helga and it found no refusal from her.
Váru þeir váttar at heitorði Þorsteins.	Were they witnesses to title Thorstein's.	There were then witnesses to Thorstein's proposal.
Þorsteinn vildi fara útan fyrst, en ráð skyldi takast, er hann kæmi aptr.	Thorstein willed travel out-of first, as advice should take, when he came back.	Thorstein wished to travel out first and advised that it would take place when he came back.
Fara þeir Þorsteinn ok Einarr, ok tekr Þorsteinn skyrbjúg í hafi, at því er þeir kalla, ok varð hann eigi liðfárr.	Travelled they Thorstein and Einar, and took Thorstein scurvy in sea, to that was they called, and was he not team-working.	Thorstein and Einar then travelled out to sea, and Thorstein took to scurvy, and he was not able to do any work for the team.
Menn hlógu at honum, ok var Einarr upphafsmaðr at því.	Men laughed to him, and was Einar instigator to that.	Men laughed at him, and Einar was the instigator of that.
Ok er þeir kómu til Nóregs, leigðu þeir þar skemmu eina, en gáfu engan gaum at Þorsteini.	And when they came to Norway, rented they there storehouse one, but gave none heed to Thorstein.	And when they came to Norway they rented a storehouse but paid no heed to Thorstein.
Hann lá þar allan vetr.	He laid there all winter.	He laid there all winter.
Einarr spottar hann mjök ok lét kveða um hann.	Einar mocked him much and let sang about him.	Einar mocked him very much, and composed verses about him.
Ok um várit hittir Einarr Þorstein ok biðr hann fjárskiptis, lézt vilja hafa einn skipit, kvað sér þykkja Þorsteinn ólíkligr til útanferðar.	And about spring met Einar Thorstein and asked him fee-exchange, let willed had alone ship, said he thought Thorstein unlikely to out-travel.	And about spring Einar met Thorstein and asked him for a deal, that he wished to have the ship alone, because he thought Thorstein was unlikely to travel out.
Þorsteinn kvað eigi fjarri því farit hafa, sem hann gat um skaplyndi Einars.	Thorstein said not away then travel had, which he got about mind Einar's.	Thorstein said that this had not gone away from what he had expected with Einar.

Old Norse	Literal	English
Þeir skipta um várit fjárhlut svá, at Einarr kaus, en Þorsteinn skipti ór rúmi sínu.	They divided about spring fee-lots so, as Einar chose, but Thorstein changed out-of room his.	About spring they divided their goods as Einar had chosen, but Thorstein did not emerge from his room.
Einarr hlaut skipit ok helt til Íslands um sumarit.	Einar got ship and held to Iceland about summer.	Einar got the ship and set sail for Iceland about summer.
Ok er hann kom at, var hann spurðr tíðenda.	And when he came back-from, was he asked news.	When he came back, he was asked for news.
En hann kvaðst eigi tíðendi kunna at segja greiðliga, kvað Þorsteinn eigi dauðan hafa verit sérliga, en þó hefði hann eigi ólíkligr verit, at hann myndi eigi aptr koma.	But he said not news knowing to say clearly, said Thorstein not dead at-sea became especially, but though would-have he not unlikely be, to he would not return come.	But he said that he did not know of any news to say clearly, saying that Thorstein was not dead at sea exactly, but he would be unlikely to return.
Einarr reið til föður síns ok svivirði mjök Þorstein í allri frásögn.	Einar rode to father his and dishonoured much Thorstein to all from-saying.	Einar rode to his father and dishonoured Thorstein in all that he said.
Um haustit kom skip af hafi í Reyðarfjörð.	About autumn came ships from sea in Reydarfjord.	About autumn ships came from sea to Reydarfjord.
Einarr reið til skips ok keypti af Austmanni, at hann segði andlát Þorsteins, ok svá gerði hann ok allir skipmenn.	Einar rode to ships and bought of Eastern-man, to he said death Thorstein's, and so made he and all ship-men.	Einar rode to the ships and bribed a Norwegian man to say that Thorstein had died, and so he did, and all the ship's men.
Einarr kom heim ok sagði andlát Þorsteins ok kvað hann hefði fengit herfiligan dauða þann vetr.	Einar came home and said death Thorstein's and said he would-have caught harrowing-like death that winter.	Einar came home and said of Thorstein's death, and said that he had caught a harrowing death at sea that winter.
5	**5**	**5**
Einarr bað föður sinn, at hann skyldi biðja Helgu Krakadóttur.	Einar asked father his, to he would ask Helga's Daughter-of-Kraka.	Einar asked his father to ask for the hand of Helga daughter of Kraka.
Þórir kvað svá vera skyldu.	Thori said so be would.	Thori said that he would.
Nú fara þeir heiman ok koma til Kraka ok vekja bónorðit við hann fyrir hönd Einars.	Now travelled they home and came to Kraki and awoke proposal with him for hand Einar's.	Now they travelled home and came to Kraki and brought up the proposal with him for Einar's hand.

Old Norse	Literal	English
Kraki kvaðst áðr vilja prófa til viss andlát Þorsteins, en lézt þá mundu gefa Einari konuna, ef þat væri áðr til víss vitat.	Kraki spoke before willed prove to know death Thorstein's, but let then would give Einar wife, if that would-be before to surely know.	Kraki said that before he wished to know for sure of Thorstein's death, but then would give Einar a wife if that was surely known before.
Þórir kvað þat eigi sannligt, at Einarr væri vánbiðill konu þeirar, er skjótt var heitin Þorsteini.	Thori said that not true-like, to Einar was hopeful woman their, that quickly was named Thorstein.	Thori said that it was unjust since Einar was so hopeful for a wife and Thorstein had been so quickly named.
Eigi lét Kraki gangast svör þessa máls.	Not let Kraki go answer this matter.	Kraki did not let the answer go on the matter.
Fara þeir feðgar heim við svá búit, ok litlu síðar ríðr Einarr norðr til Hofs ok segir Þorgilsi bónorðit ok kveðr sér hafa verit neitat.	Travel they father-and-son home therefore so dwelling, and little afterwards rode Einar north to Hof and told Thorgils's marriage-proposal and said that had been denied.	Then father and son travelled home to their dwellings, and a little afterwards Einar rode north to Hof and told Thorgils about the marriage proposal and how it had been denied.
Hrani var hjá ok svaraði svá:	Hrani was beside and answered so:	Hrani was beside him and answered thus:
"Illa kom þér, Einarr, í hald góðir frændr, ef þú skalt eigi fá konu í þessa, kvað honum ok lítil stoða at vera í vináttu við Þorgils, ef hann skyldi einskis meta þessa sneypu, er Einari var ger.	"Ill comes to-you, Einar, if hold good kinsmen, if you shall not get woman of this, said he and little stood to be in friendship with Thorgils, if he would not appreciate this shame, that Einar was made.	"It comes badly to you Einar that you hold good kinsmen if you shall not get this woman", he said, and there is little standing in your friendship with Thorgils if he would not appreciate the shame that Einar was made.
Þorgils svarar:	Thorgils answered:	Thorgils answered:
"Mér virðist Kraki vitrliga með fara, ok munda ek svá gera, ef ek ætta hans hlut.	"To-me seems Kraki wise-like with go, and would I so do, if I had his share.	"It seems to me that Kraki is wise to go with this, and I would do so if I had his share".
Satt eitt sagði Einarr frá orðum Kraka, en þó eggjaði Hrani Þorgils at fara með honum.	Truth alone said Einar from words Kraki, but though urged Hrani Thorgils to travel with him.	Einar spoke the truth alone about Kraki's words, but though Hrani urged Thorgils to travel with him.
Þorgils kvað eigi létt hugr um segja, þó at þessu ráði yrði komit í hendr honum.	Thorgils said not let thought about to-say, though to this advice would come to hands his.	Thorgils said that he was not inclined to give advice, though the matter was in his hands.

Old Norse	Literal	English
Síðan fóru þeir ok hittu Kraka, ok hafði hann in sömu svör fyrir sér sem fyrr.	Afterwards went they and met Kraki, and had he the same answer for as was before.	Afterwards they went and met Kraki, and he had the same answer as before.
Þorgils mælti þá:	Thorgils said then:	Thorgils then said:
"Vera má, at þú ráðir dóttur þinni, en eigi muntu svá undan setja, at þú fáir eigi sakargiptir um annat.	"Be may, to you advise daughter yours, but not shall so under sit, to you few not sake-given about anything-else.	"It may be that you advise your daughter, but you won't do it in such a way that you won't be penalised for anything else".
Kraki mælti:	Kraki said:	Kraki said:
"Eigi mun ek til þess hætta.	"Not will I to this leave.	"I do not wish to leave it to this".
Hann fastnaði þá dóttur sína Einari ok hafði sjálfr brúðkaup inni.	He betrothed then daughter his Einar and had himself wedding the.	He then betrothed his daughter to Einar, and hosted the wedding himself.
Kraki skyldi vera ór öllum vanda um kaupbrigði við Þorstein.	Kraki should be out-of all problems about bargains with Thorstein.	Kraki was released of all issues regarding the agreements with Thorstein.
6	6	6
Þat er nú frá Þorsteini at segja, at honum batnaði,	That is now from Thorstein to say, to he improved,	It is now to say from Thorstein that his health improved.
ok bjó hann skip sitt til Íslands ok kom at næsta sumar eptir brúðkaupit í Reyðarfjörð ok hafði selt Aust mönnum skipit.	and prepared he ship his to Iceland and came to next summer after wedding in Reydarfjord and had sold Eastern men ship.	He prepared his ship to go to Iceland and came out the following summer after the wedding in Reydarfjord, and had sold his ship to Norwegians.
Hann ætlaði til ráðahagsins við Helgu ok láta af förum.	He intended to consult with Helga's and leave of travel.	He intended to consult with Helga, and take his leave of any more travelling.
Ok er hann kom til Íslands, frétti hann alla þessa ráðabreytni.	And when he came to Iceland, heard he all this decision-conduct.	And when he came to Iceland he heard all about the conduct.
Fór hann þá til fundar við föður sinn ok let þó haldast skipsöluna eigi at síðr.	Travelled he then to meet with father his and let though held ship's-sale none to less.	Then he travelled to meet with his father, and held to the sale of his ship none the less.

Old Norse	Literal	English
Þorsteinn lét lítt á sér finna um þetta mál.	Thorstein let little of this found about the matter.	Thorstein let little be known of how he found the matter.
Hann keypti sér skip um vetrinn, er uppi stóð í Bolungarhöfn, ok bjó at öllu.	He bought himself ship about winter, which up stood in Bolungarhof, and prepared to all.	He bought himself another ship about winter, which stood up in Bolungarhof, and prepared it for all.
Bræðr hans ætluðu með honum útan ok urðu eigi búnir svá skjótt sem hann, því at þeir fóru at fjárheimtingum sínum um heraðit.	Brothers his intended with him out-of and became not prepared so quickly as he, because to they went to finances theirs about district.	His brothers intended to travel out with him, but were not prepared so quickly, because they went about the district calling in their debts.
Austmenn vesuðust illa, er þeir þurftu at bíða, bræðra Þorsteins, ef byrr kæmi á.	Eastern-men felt badly, if they needed to wait, brothers Thorstein's, if fair-wind came to.	The Norwegians felt bad that they needed to wait for Thorstein's brothers, even though there was a favourable wind.
Þorsteinn mælti þá:	Thorstein said then:	Then Thorstein said:
"Ek mun ríða frá skipi váru ok hitta þá ok biðja þá, at þeir flýti sér, en þér skuluð bíða mín it skemmsta sjau nætr.	"I will ride from ship ours and meet then and ask then, to they hurry themselves, but you should wait for-me the shortest seven nights.	"I will ride from our ship and meet them then, and ask that they hurry themselves, but you shoulld wait for me at least seven nights".
Þorsteinn reið útan eptir Öxarfirði ok í Bolungarhöfn ok upp á Möðrudalsheiði ok ofan til Vápnafjarðar ok svá austr yfir Smjörvatnsheiði ok austr yfir Jökulsá at brú ok svá yfir Fljótsdalsheiði ok austr yfir Lagarfljót ok upp með fljótinu unz hann kom í Atlavik snemma morgins.	Thorstein rode out after Oxarfjord and of Bolungarhof and up to Modrudalsheidi and down to Vopnafjord and so east over Smjorvatnsheidi and east over Jokulsla to bridge and so over Fljotsdalsheidi and east over Lagarfljot and up with river until he came to Atlavik early morning.	Thorsteinn rode out along Oxarfjord from Bolungarhof and up to Modrudalsheidi and down to Vopnafjord and so east over Smjorvatnsheidi and so over Fljotsdalsheidi and east over Lagarfljot and up along the river until he came to Atlavik early in the morning.
Þórir var farinn í skóg ok húskarlar hans með honum ofan á Bolungarvöllu.	Thori was travelling to forest and house-carls his with him over to Bolungarvollu.	Thorir was traveling to the forest with his house-carls over to Bolungarvollu.
Einarr var heima ok var eigi upp risinn, er Þorsteinn kom at durunum.	Einar was home and was not up risen, when Thorstein came to door.	Einar was home and had not yet risen when Thorstein came to the door.
Kona var úti, er Ósk hét.	Woman was about, who Osk named.	There was a woman there named Osk.

Old Norse	Literal	English
Hon spurði, hverr inn komni maðr væri.	She asked, who then coming man was.	She asked who the man who had come was.
Þorsteinn svarar:	Thorstein answered:	Thorstein answered:
"Sigurðr heiti ek, ok á ek at gjalda Einari skuld, ok vil ek nú afhenda honum, ok gakk þú inn ok vek Einar ok bið hann út ganga.	"Sigurd named i, and am I to debt Einar should, and will I not of-hand him, and go you then and wake Einar and ask him out going.	"I am named Sigurd and I should give my debt to Einar, and I wish to hand to him now, go you then and wake Einar up and ask him to come out".
Þorsteinn hafði spjót í hendi ok ullhött á höfði.	Thorstein had spear in hand and woolen-hat on head.	Thorstein had a spear in his hand and a woolen hat on his head.
Konan vakti Einar.	Woman awoke Einar.	The woman awoke Einar.
Hann spurði, hverr kominn væri.	He asked, who came was.	He asked who had come.
Hon sagði, at hann nefndist Sigurðr.	She said, to he named Sigurd.	She said that he was named Sigurd.
Einarr stóð þá upp ok kippti skóm á fætr sér ok tók skikkju yfir sik ok gekk út síðan.	Einar stood then up and snatched shoes on feet his and took cloak over himself and went out afterwards.	Einar then stood up and snatched shoes on his feet, and took a cloak over himself and went out afterwards.
Ok er hann kom at, kenndi hann Einarr, at þar var kominn Þorsteinn, ok varð Einarr nökkut fár við.	And when he came out, knew he Einar, to there was come Thorstein, and became Einar somewhat unresponsive with.	And when he came out Einar knew that Thorstein had come and Einar became unresponsive.
Þorsteinn mælti:	Thorstein spoke:	Thorstein spoke:
"Því em ek hér kominn, at ek vil vita, hverju þú villt bæta mér, er þú gabbaðir skyrbjúg minn í hafi ok hlótt at mér með hásetum þínum, ok mun ek vera alllítilþægr at.	"Because am I here come, to I will know, how you will compensate me, as you mocked scurvy mine at sea and laughed to me with crew yours, and shall I be all-little-quiet at.	"Because I have come here, I wish to know how you will compensate me for how you mocked me when I had scurvy at sea and laughed at me with your crew, and I shall be quiet".
Einarr mælti:	Einar spoke:	Einar spoke:
"Heimtu fyrst at öllum, er hlógu at þér,	"Demand first to all, who laughed to you,	"Demand first from all those who laughed at you.
ok mun ek bæta þér, ef allir bæta aðrir.	and will I compensate you, if all compensate others.	I will then compensate you if all others compensate".

Old Norse	Literal	English
Þorsteinn segir:	Thorstein told:	Thorstein answered:
"Ek em ekki svá féþurfi, at ek nenna alla at skja, en ek vil þú bætir fyrir þik.	"I am not so fee-needing, to I care all to seek, but I will you compensate for you.	"I am not so much in need of money that I care at all to seek, and I wish that you compensate for you".
Einarr kveðst eigi bæta mundu, ok sneri hann undan ok til svefnskemmunnar.	Einar said not compensate would, and turned he away and to sleeping-room.	Einar said that he would not compensate and he turned away to go to his room.
Þorsteinn bað hann bíða ok hrapa eigi svá skjótt til rekkjunnar Helgu.	Thorstein bid him wait and hurried not so quickly to bed Helga's.	Thorstein bid him wait, and not hurry so quickly to Helga's bed.
Einarr gaf engan gaum at því, er hann mælti.	Einar gave none heed to then, as he spoke.	Einar gave no need to him then as he spoke.
Síðan lagði Þorsteinn á Einari með spjótinu ok í gegnum hann.	Afterwards laid Thorstein on Einar with spear and to through him.	Afterwards Thorstein laid towards Einar with a spear and it went through him.
Einarr fell dauðr inn í skemmuna.	Einar fell dead in about sleeping-room.	Einar fell dead into the room.
Þorsteinn bað griðkonuna at greiða ferð Einars.	Thorstein asked house-maiden to assistance travel Einar's.	Thorstein asked the house maiden to speed Einar on his way.
Þorsteinn ríðr þá ina sömu leið aptr ok hann reið fram.	Thorstein rode then the same way back and he rode from.	Thorstein then rode the same way back as he had rode from.
Hann reið vestr yfir háls til sels Þorbjarnar, er stóð á milli Melrakkasléttu ok Ormsár.	He rode west across hills to shed Thorbjorn's, which stood on between Melrakkasletta and Ormsa.	He rode west across the hills to Thorbjorn's shed which stood in between Melrakkasletta and Ormsa.
Hann spurði Þorbjörn, ef bræðr hans hefði þar komit, en Þorbjörn kvað þat eigi vera.	He asked Thorbjorn, if brothers his would-have there come, but Thorbjorn said that not been.	He asked thorbjorn if his brothers had come out there, but Thorbjorn said they had not been.
Þorsteinn sagði honum tíðendin ok bað hann segja bræðrum sínum, at þeir flýtti sér til skips.	Thorstein told him news and bid he tell brothers his, to they hurry themselves to ship.	Thorstein told him the news and bid that he tell his brothers, that they hurry themselves to the ship.
Reið Þorsteinn þá til skips.	Rode Thorstein then to ship.	Then Thorstein rode to the ship.

Old Norse	Literal	English
Griðkona gerði honum Þóri orð ok lét segja honum víg Einars, sonar síns, ok brá Þórir skjótt við ok fór norðr til Vápnafjarðar með tvá húskarla sína ok fór á skipi yfir fljót ok til Hofs.	The-house-keeper gave him Thori word and let tell him killing Einar's, son his, and startled Thori quickly with and travelled north to Vopnafjord with two house-carls his and travelled by ship across river and to Hof.	The housekeeper sent word to Thori and told him about the killing of his son Einar, and Thori was quick and traveled north to Vopnafjord with two of his house-carls and travelled by ship across the river and to Hof.
Sagði hann þeim Hofsmönnum víg Einars.	Told he the Men-of-Hof killing Einar's.	He told the men of Hof about Einar's killing.
Þorgils kvað sér eigi vel hafa hugr um sagt, þegar er Einarr fekk Helgu.	Thorgils said he not well have thought about said, when that Einar married Helga.	Thorgils said that he did not think well of when it was said thast Einar married Helga.
Þeir báðu hann eptir ríða.	They bid him after ride.	They bid him to ride after them.
Hann lét þá taka hesta sína.	He had then take horses theirs.	He then had his horses fetched.
Hrani frýði honum áðr hugar, ef hann seinkaði ferðinni.	Hrani persuaded him about mind, if he delayed travelling.	Hrani persuaded him about his thoughts if he delayed travelling.
Þórir hvarf aptr ok gerði þat at ráði Þorgils, en húskarlar hans fóru með Þorgilsi, ok váru þeir sjau saman ok fóru síðan leið sína.	Thori disappeared again and did that to advice Thorgils, but house-carls his went with Thorgils's, and were they seven together and travelled afterwards way theirs.	Thori disappeared again and did as Thorgils had advised him, but his house-carls went with Thorgils and they were seven together, and afterwards they travelled on their way.
7	7	7
Bræðr Þorsteins ríða til sels Þorbjarnar annan daginn eptir, er Þorsteinn hafði þaðan riðit.	Brothers Thorstein's rode to shed Thorbjorn's next day after, that Thorstein had from-there rode.	Thorstein's brothers rode to Thorbjorn's shed the next day after Thorstein had ridden away.
Þar höfðu þeir dagverð, en lögðust síðan niðr til svefns.	There had they time-of-day-meal, but laid afterwards down to sleep.	They had their breakfast but then afterwards laid down to sleep.
Þorbjörn latti þá þess mjök, því at hann sagði þeim víg Einars ok orðsending Þorsteins, en Þorbjörn var vinr hvárratveggja.	Thorbjorn discouraged then this much, because to he told them killing Einar's and message Thorstein's, but Thorbjorn was friend either-side.	Thorbjorn discouraged this greatly because he told them of Einar's killing, and Thorstein's message, and was a friend on either side.

Old Norse	Literal	English
Litlu síðar kom Þorgils ok þeir sjau saman.	Little afterwards came Thorgils and they seven together.	A little afterwards Thorgils came with his men, and they were seven together.
Þorbjörn sagði þeim bræðrum, at þeir Þorgils váru þar komnir, ok vakti hann þá.	Thorbjorn told they brothers, to they Thorgils were there coming, and awoke he then.	Thorbjorn told them brothers that Thorgils and his men were coming and he awoke them.
Hvergi máttu þeir undan komast.	Nowhere could they away-from come.	There was nowhere they could go to get away.
Þorbjörn réð þeim þat, at þeir grafi þar djúpa gröf í selinu fyrir durunum, en ek mun standa í durunum.	Thorbjorn advised them that, to they dig there deep ditch about shed before door, but I will stand about door.	Thorbjorg advised them that they dig a deep trench around the shed before the door, "but I will stand in front of the door".
Ok svá gerðu þeir.	And so did they.	And so they did.
Þeir Þorgils koma þá at selinu.	They Thorgils came then to shed.	Thorgils and his men then came to the shed.
Þóttust þeir vita, at þeir bræðr myndi þar inni, er hrossin váru þar mdd ok nýkomin undan klyfjum.	Thought they knew, to they brothers would there in, be horses were there tired and newly-arrived under hooves.	They thought they knew that the brothers were inside, because the horses were tired and newly unsaddled.
Veit ek, segir Þorgils, at þeir eru hér.	Know i, said Thorgils, to they are here.	"I know", said Thorgils, "that they are here".
Þorbjörn svarar:	Thorbjorn answered:	Thorbjorn answered:
"Þú ert maðr glöggvastr, en þó eru þeir brðr eigi hér, sem þú segir,	"You are man sharpest, but though are they brothers not here, as you say,	"You are the sharpest of men, but though the brothers are not here as you say.
en ek lét fara eptir viðum hross mín, ok höfum nýtekit af þeim klyfjar.	but I let travel after wood horses mine, and have newly-taken of them hoof.	But I travelled to get wood with my horses, and I have just taken off their hooves.
Eru þau nýkomin frá vetrhúsum, en áðr gengu þau af rekaströndum til skálagerðar í Sveinungsvík ok á ek hrossin.	Are they newly-come from winter-house, but before went they of rekastrondum to hut-make about Sveinungsvik and are I horses.	They are newly come from the winter house, and before that they were on Rekastrondum to make a hut, and they are my horses".
Þorgils kvaðst eigi þessu trúa mundu, ok far þú ór durunum, ok viljum vér rannsaka selit.	Thorgils said not this trusted should, and go you out-from door, and will we search shed.	Thorgils said that he did not trust this "and you get away from the door, and we will search the shed".

Old Norse	Literal	English
Þorbjörn kvaðst þat eigi gera mundu, síðan þér trúið eigi minni tilsögu.	Thorbjorn said that not done would-be, since you trust not less to-say.	Thorbjorm said that it would not be done "since you will not trust what I say".
Hrani mælti:	Hrani spoke:	Hrani spoke:
"Drepum hann, ef hann vill eigi fara or durunum.	"Kill-we him, if he will not go out-from door.	"Let us kill him if he will not go away from the door".
Þorgils svarar:	Thorgils answered:	Thorgils answered:
"Þá þykkir föður mínum illa.	"Then think father mine badly.	"Then my father would think badly about that".
Þá bauð Þorkell flettir at fara á bak húsinu ok hlaupa af vegginum ofan milli Þorbjarnar ok duranna ok bera hann svá frá durunum ofan fyrir brekkuna.	Then offered Thorkell Fleecer to go to back of-the-house and jump of roof above between Thorbjorn and the-door and bear him so from the-door over for slope.	Then Thorkell Fleecer offered to go to to the back of the house and jump off the roof above, between Thorbjorn and the-door, and bear him from the door and over the slope.
Þorgils bað hann svá gera.	Thorgils bid him so do.	Thorgils bid him to do so.
Síðan breytti Þorkell svá, at Þorbjörn varð með þessari atferð borinn frá selsdurunum.	After changed Thorkell so, to Thorbjorn became with this method carried away shed-door.	Afterwards Thorkell changed so that Thorbjorn was carried away from the hut door.
Síðan bundu þeir hann.	After bound they him.	Afterwards they bound him.
Eptir þat gengu þeir at durunum, ok mátust þeir um, hverr þeira skyldi fyrstr inn ganga.	After that went they to door, and discussed they about, who of-them should first in go.	After that they went to the doors and argued which of them should go in first.
En er Þorgils fann þetta, mælti hann:	But when Thorgils found this, spoke he:	But when Þorgils found this he spoke:
"Eigi verðr oss nú hugmannliga er vér þorum eigi inn at ganga".	"Not become we now intelligent as we dare not to go in".	"We will not be wise now if we do not dare to enter".
Þorgils hleypr þá inn.	Thorgils ran then in.	Thorgils then ran in.
Þorbjörn aftalði hann ok sagðist letja hann inn at ganga, en hann gaf engan gaum at orðum hans.	Thorbjorn of-told him and said discourage he in to go, but he gave none heed to words his.	Þorbjörn dissuaded him and said he would discourage him to enter, but he paid no attention to his words.

Old Norse	Literal	English
Hann hafði skjöldinn yfir höfði sér.	He had shield over head his.	He had a shield over his head.
Hann snarar þá inn ok hljóp í gröfina, ok drápu þeir brðr hann þar í gröfinni.	He sneaked then in and ran to ditch, and killed they brothers him there in the-grave.	He then snuck in and ran into the ditch, and the brothers killed him there in the tomb.
Síðan rufu förunautar Þorgils selit ok sóttu þá brðr um stundar sakir.	Afterwards tore companions Thorgils shed and sought then brothers about awhile sake.	Afterwards Thorgil's companions tore their way into the shed and pursued the brothers for a while.
Hrani gullhöttr lá á selvegginum ok koglaði þann veg inn.	Hrani gold-hat lay about shed-ways and quivered he way in.	Hrani Gold Hat kay along the shed walls and found a way in.
Þá var hann lagðr spjóti í höndina.	Then was he laid spear in hand.	Then he had a spear in his hand.
Þeir brðr vörðust bæði vel ok drengiliga, ok fellu báðir þar at síðustu með góðan orðstír.	They brothers guarded both well and fellow-like, and fell both there to finally with good reputation.	The brothers both defended themselves wel, but then fell there finally with good reputation.
Þar fellu ok báðir húskarlar Þóris ok inn þriðji maðr, Þorgils Þorsteins son, er þá var þrítugr at aldri.	There fell and both house-carls Thorir and then third man, Thorgils son-of-Thorstein son, as then was thirty to age.	There two house-carls of Thorir also fell, and Thorgils son of Thorstein, who was then thirty in age.
Þorbjörn var leystr síðan eptir fundinn.	Thorbjorn was loosened since after found.	Thorbjorn was released afterwards.
Hann frði alla vöru þeira í Bolungarhöfn til skips ok sagði Þorsteini tíðendin.	He took all wares theirs in Bolungarhof to ship and said Thorstein news.	He took all of the brothers' belongings to the ship in Bolungarhof and told Thorstein the news.
Þorsteinn kvað Þorbjörn þetta vel gert hafa, ok skiljast með mikilli vináttu.	Thorstein said Thorbjorn that well done had, and separated with much friendship.	Thorstein said that Thorbjorn had done well and they separated with good friendship.
8	**8**	**8**
Þorsteinn fór útan um sumarit ok var á burt fimm vetr.	Thorstein went out-of about summer and was to away five winters.	Thorstein went abroad that summer and was away for five winters.

The Saga of Thorstein the White (Old Norse)

Old Norse	Literal	English
Hann kom sér vel við höfðingja ok þótti inn röskvasti maðr.	He came himself well with chieftans and thought then most-mature man.	He had the favour of the chieftains and was thought of as the most mature man.
Hrani gullhöttr kom heim til Hofs ok sagði Þorsteini hvíta, at synir Þorfinns tveir væri fallnir ok húskarlar Þóris tveir.	Hrani gold-hat came home to Hof and told Thorstein white, to sons Thorfin's two would-be fallen and house-carls Thorir two.	Hrani Gold-Hat came home to Hof and told Thorstein the White that Thorfin's two sons were fallen and Thorir's two house-carls.
Þorsteinn spurði hann:	Thorstein asked he:	Thorstein asked:
"Hvar er Þorgils, sonr minn?"	"Where is Thorgils, son mine?"	"Where is my son Thorgils?"
Hrani svarar:	Hrani answered:	Hrani answered:
"Hann er ok fallinn líka.	"He was and fallen alike.	"He was also fallen".
Þorsteinn mælti:	Thorstein said:	Thorstein said:
"Fjándliga segir þú frá tíðendum.	"Fiendishly say you from news.	"You bring fiendish news.
Illt hefir jafnan af þér hlotizt ok þínum ráðum.	Ill has equally of your lot and your advice.	Ill has always been your lot and your advice".
Þetta þótti mönnum mikil tíðendi, þá er spurðust.	That seemed men much news, then was learned-of.	It seemed much when people learned the news of it.
Um sumarit eptir váru mál til búin á hendr Þorsteini Þorfinnssyni, ok varð hann sekr um víg Einars.	About summer after were matters to prepared at hand Thorstein son-of-Thorfin, and became he guilty about killing Einar's.	About the following summer, a case was prepared against Thorstein son of Thorfin, and he was found guilty of Einar's killing.
Brodd-Helgi var þá þrévetr, er faðir hans var drepinn, ok var þá þegar efniligr maðr at jöfnum aldri.	Brodd-Helgi was then three-winters, when father his was killed, and was then already promising man to equal age.	Spike-Helgi was then three winters old when his father was kiled, and was then already a promising for his age.
Þorsteinn Þorfinnsson fór til Íslands at fimm vetr um liðnum ok kom skipi sínu í Miðfjörð.	Thorstein son-of-Thorfin travelled to Iceland to five winters about passed and came ship his to Midfjord.	Thorstein son-of-Thorgin travelled to Iceland five winters later, and his ship came to Mifdjord.
Hann reið þegar norðr til Hofs við fimmta mann.	He rode then north to Hof with five men.	He rode then north to Hof with five men.

Old Norse	Literal	English
Brodd-Helgi var þá átta vetra gamall ok lék sér á hlaði úti ok bauð þeim öllum þar at vera.	Brodd-Helgi was then eight winters old and played he about farmyard outside and invited them all there to be.	Spike-Helgi was then eight winters old and he played about the farmyard outside and invited them all in.
Þorsteinn spurði, hví hann laðaði gesti.	Thorstein asked, why he attracted guests.	Thorstein asked how it was that he invited guests.
Hann kvaðst þar allt eiga með afa sínum.	He spoke there all owned with grandfather his.	He spoke that all there was owned by his grandfather.
Þeir Þorsteinn Þorfinnsson gengu inn eptir þat.	They Thorstein son-of-Thorfin went in after that.	Thorstein son-of-Thorfin and his men went in after that.
Þorsteinn hvíti kenndi farmannadaun ok spurði, hverir komnir væri.	Thorstein white knew farmers-death and asked, why came were.	Thorstein the White knew of the farmers death and asked why they had come.
Þorsteinn Þorfinnsson segir it sanna.	Thorstein son-of-Thorfin said the truth.	Thorstein son-of-Thorgin told him the truth.
Þorsteinn hvíti mælti:	Thorstein white spoke:	Thorstein the White spoke:
"Hvárt þótti þér of lítil mín skapraun, ef þú sóttir mik eigi heim, blindan karl ok gamlan?"	"Either thought you of little my temperament, if you sought me not home, blind man and old?"	"Either you thought little of my trials, if you sought me at home, a blind old man".
Þorsteinn Þorfinnsson svarar:	Thorstein son-of-Thorfin answered:	Thorstein son-of-Thorfin answered:
"Eigi gekk mér þat til, heldr hitt, at ek vil bjóða þér sjálfdmi fyrir Þorgils, son þinn, ok hefi ek rit góz til þess at bta hann, svá at engi hafi annarr maðr dýrri verit.	"Not going to-me that to, rather other, to I will bid you self-example for Thorgils, son yours, and have I considerable estate to this to compensate he, so to none had another man precious made.	This was not my thought, rather the opposite, that I wish to bid you self-judgement for Thorgils, your son, and I have considerable estate for this to compensate for him, so much that no other man has been paid".
Þorsteinn hvíti kvaðst eigi vilja bera Þorgils, son sinn, í sjóði.	Thorstein white spoke not will bear Thorgils, son his, to funds.	Thorstein the White said that he did not wish to bear his son Thorgil in his purse.
Þorsteinn Þorfinnsson ok var kallaðr inn fagri.	Thorstein son-of-Thorfin and was called then fair.	Thorstein son of Thorfin was called Thorstein the Fair.
Hann sprettr þá upp ok leggr höfuð sitt í kné Þorsteini hvíta, nafna sínum.	He sprang then up and laid head his about knee Thorstein white, namesake his.	He jumped then up and laid his head on the knee of Thorstein the White, his namesake.

The Saga of Thorstein the White (Old Norse)

Old Norse	Literal	English
Þorsteinn hvíti svarar þá:	Thorstein white answered then:	Thorstein the White then answered:
"Eigi vil ek láta höfuð sitt af hálsi slá.	"Not will I let head his off neck struck.	"I will not let your head be struck from your neck".
Munu þar eyru smst, er óxu.	Shall then ears same, was grow.	Your ears will become you better where they grow.
En þá geri ek sætt okkar á millum, at þú skalt fara hingat til Hofs til umsýslu með allt þitt, ok vera hér, meðan ek vil, en þú sel skip þitt.	But then make I settlement ours on between, to you shall travel here to Hof to administrations with all yours, and be here, with I will, but you sell ship yours.	But then I make this our settlement, that you shall travel here to Hof with all your people, and be here as long as I am, having sold your ship.
Þessari sætt játar Þorsteinn fagri,	This settlement accepts Thorstein fair,	Thorstein the Fair accepted this settlement.
ok er þeir kumpánar kómu út, lék sveinninn Helgi Þorgilsson sér at gullreknu spjóti, er Þorsteinn fagri hafði sett hjá durunum, er hann gekk inn.	and as they companions came out, played boy Helgi son-of-Thorgils with to gold-plated spear, as Thorstein fair had set beside door, as he went in.	And as Thorstein and his companions went outside, the boy Helgi son of Thorgil played with a gold plated spear that was set beside the door when he went in.
Þorsteinn fagri mælti við Helga:	Thorstein fair spoke with Helga:	Thorstein the Fair spoke with Helga.
"Villtu þiggja af mér spjótit?"	"Will-you accept of my spear?"	"Will you accept my spear?"
Helgi réðst þá um við Þorstein hvíta, fóstra sinn, hvárt hann skyldi þiggja spjótit at Þorsteini fagra.	Helgi decided then about with Thorstein white, foster his, whether he should receive spear of Thorstein fair.	Helgi then decided about this with Thorstein the White's foster father whether he should accept the spear of Thorstein the Fair.
Þorsteinn hvíti svarar ok bað hann þiggja víst ok launa sem bezt.	Thorstein white answered and bid he receive certainly and repay as best.	Thorstein the White answered, inviting him to certainly receive and repay the gift as best he could.
Þorsteinn fagri var eina nátt á Hofi í þat sinni.	Thorstein fair was one night about Hof about that his.	Thorstein the Fair was in Hof for one night on that occasion.
Þorsteinn fagri fór til skips síns ok seldi þat.	Thorstein fair travelled to ship his and sold it.	Thorstein the Fair travelled to his ship and sold it.

Old Norse	Literal	English
Síðan frði hann sik til Hofs í Vápnafjörð með allt sitt.	Afterwards took he himself to Hof in Vopnafjord with all his.	Afterwards he took himself to Hof in Vopnafjord with all his companions.
Hann frði mjök fram kvikfé Þorsteins hvíta, nafna síns.	He took much from wealth Thorstein's white, namesake his.	He greatly advanced the wealth of his namesake, Thorstein the White.
En er hann hafði þar verit nökkura stund, þá vildi Þorsteinn hvíti, at Þorsteinn, nafni hans, bæði Helgu Krakadóttur, ok svá gerði hann.	And as he had there been some while, then willed Thorstein white, to Thorstein, namesake his, both Helga's Daughter-of-Kraka, and so did he.	And when he had been there for some time, Thorstein the White willed his namesake to ask for the hand of Helga daughter of Kraka, and so he did.
Þorsteinn hvíti var í ferð með honum, ok gengu þau mál vel fram, ok þótti Kraka þetta gert eptir sínu skaplyndi.	Thorstein white was about journey with him, and went then matter well from, and thought Kraki that made after his temperament.	Thorstein the White journeyed with him, and the matter went well, with Kraki finding it well with his liking.
Fór Helga þá til Hofs með Þorsteini fagra, því at Þorsteinn hvíti vildi brúðkaup inni hafa, því at hann þóttist hrumr til at fara at skja brúñkaupit annars staðar, ok af því var svá gert.	Travelled Helga then to Hof with Thorstein fair, since to Thorstein white willed wedding the at-sea, since to he thought decrepit to that travel to seek wedding another place, and of then was so done.	Helga then went to Hof with Thorstein the Fair because Thorstein the White wanted the wedding inside, because he thought it was too late to attend the wedding elsewhere, and so it was done.
Boðit fór vel fram.	Invitation went well from.	The invitation went well.
Váru samferðir þeira góðar.	Was interaction theirs good.	Their interaction was good.
Átta vetr var Þorsteinn fagri at Hofi með nafna sínum ok var honum í sonar stað í allri umsýslu.	Eight winters was Thorstein fair to Hof with namesake his and was him his son's place about all administered.	For eight winters Thorstein the Fair was at Hof with his namesake, and was a son to him in all his dealings.
Ok þá er svá var komit tímum, mælti Þorsteinn hvíti til nafna síns:	And then was so was come time, spoke Thorstein white to namesake his:	And when the time had come, Thorstein the White said to his namesake:
"Vel hefir þú gefizt mér, ok ertu röskr maðr ok drengr góðr um alla hluti ok vel at þér búinn.	"Well have you given me, and are-you strong man and fellow good about all things and well to you prepared.	"Well you have given yourself to me and you are a strong man and a good man in all things and well done.

Old Norse	Literal	English
Nú vil ek, at þú bregðir þessu ráði ok svá föður þíns ok Kraka, mágs þíns, ok ráðizt allir til útanferðar með allt þat, er þér eigið, því at ek ætla Helga, frænda mínum ok fóstra, gerast mjök þungt til þín,	Now wish i, to you action this advice and so father yours and Kraki, brother-in-law yours, and advise all to out-travel with all it, as you own, because to I suppose Helga, kinsman mine and fosterer, will-be much unhappy to you,	Now I wish that you action this advice, your father, and Kraki your father-in-law. I advise you to all travel out with all that you own, because Helgi my kinsman and foster son will be very unhappy towards you.
en hann er nú átján vetra gamall,	but he is now eighteen winters old,	But he is now eighteen winters old.
en þat er líkast, at ek verða maðr ekki langlífr heðan af, en ek vilda, at vit skilðim vel, en Helgi, frændi minn, mun verða ofsamaðr mikill ok engi jafnaðarmaðr.	but that was like, to I be man not long-life from-here of, but I will, to with parted well, but Helgi, kinsman mine, will be over-bearing-man much and none equally-man.	But it seems that I will not be a long-lived man from now on, but I would like us to get along well, but my kinisman Helgi will be a great overbearing man and not an equal man.
Nú haf þú mitt ráð um þetta ok ver hér eigi lengr en ek legg ráð til.	Now have you mine advice about this and be here no longer than I lay advice to.	Now that you have my advice about this, be here no longer than I advise you to".
Þorsteinn fagri kvað svá vera skyldu.	Thorstein fair said so be should.	Thorstein the Fair said that so it should be.
Þorsteinn fagri keypti tvau skip ok fór útan með allt sitt skuldalið.	Thorstein fair bought two ships and travelled out-of with all his indebted.	Thorstein the Fair bought two ships and travelled abroad with all of his kinsmen.
Þorfinnr, faðir hans, fór ok útan ok Kraki, mágr hans.	Thorfin, father his, travelled and out-of and Kraki, brother-in-law his.	Thorfin his father travelled out, and his brother in law Kraki.
Þeir kómu norðarliga við Nóreg ok fóru um sumarit eptir norðr á Hálogaland ok ílendust þar með öllu liði sínu.	They came northerly with Norway and travelled about summer after north to Halogaland and landed then with all company theirs.	They came to the north of Norway and travelled about the summer after to Halogaland and landed then with all their company.
Bjó Þorsteinn fagri þar, meðan hann lifði, ok þótti inn vaskasti maðr.	Lived Thorstein fair there, long-as he lived, and thought-of then boldest man.	Thorstein the Fair lived there as long as he lived, and was thought of as the boldest man.
9	9	9
Helgi óx upp með Þorsteini hvíta, fóstra sínum.	Helgi grew up with Thorstein white, foster his.	Helgi grew up with Thorstein the White, his foster father.

Old Norse	Literal	English
Hann gerðist mikill maðr ok sterkr, bráðgerr, vænn ok stórmannligr ok ekki málugr í barnæsku, ódæll ok óvæginn þegar á unga aldri.	He became great man and strong, quick, kind and great-man-like and not talkative in childhood, unruly and ruthless already at young age.	He became a great and strong man, quick, kind, and generous, and not talkative in childhood, unruly and ruthless at a young age.
Hann var hugkvæmr ok margbreytinn.	He was resourceful and many-varied.	He was resourceful in many varied ways.
Þat var einn dag at Hofi, naut váru at stöðli.	That was one day to Hof, bulls were to standing.	It was one day at Hof when bulls were at the cowshed,
Þar var griðungr kominn til nautanna, mikill ok stórr.	There was bull coming to bull, great and large.	there one bull came, great and large.
Annarr griðungr var heima fyrir, mikill ok ógurligr, er þeir frændr áttu.	Another bull was home before, great and formidable, as they kinsmen had.	Another bull was at the homestead, great and formidable, belonging to the kinsmen.
Helgi var þá úti staddr ok sá, at griðungarnir gengust at ok stönguðust, ok varð heimagriðungrinn vanhluta fyrir búigriðunginum.	Helgi was then about standing and saw, to bulls went to and stabbing, and was home-bulls part for farm-bulls.	Helgi was standing outside and saw that the bulls went to and stabbed each other, the homestead bull and the farm bull.
En er Helgi sér þat, gengr hann inn ok skir sér mann brodda stóra ok bindr þá framan í ennit á heimagriðunginum.	But as Helgi saw it, went he in and fetched himself man shaft great and tied then in-front-of the head of home-bull.	But as Helgi saw it, he went in and fetched himself a great spike and tied it to the forehead of the homestead bull.
Síðan taka þeir til ok stangast sem áðr, allt þar til er heimagriðungrinn stangar hinn til dauðs.	Afterwards took they to and stabbed as before, all there until was home-bull stabbed him to death.	After this they took to stabbing each other as before, all until the homestead bull stabbed the other bull to death.
Höfðu mannbroddarnir gengit á hol.	Had spear gone into hole.	The spear had gone into a hole.
Þótti flestum mönnum þetta vera bellibragð, er Helgi hafði gert.	Thought most people that had-been trick, was Helgi had done.	Most people thought that this was a trick that Helgi had played.
Fekk hann af þessu viðrnefni ok var kallaðr Brodd-Helgi, en þat þótti þá mönnum miklu heillavænligra at hafa tvau nöfn.	Got he of this nickname and was called Brodd-Helgi, but that thought then people much beneficial to have two names.	From this he got the nickname and was called Spike-Helgi, but then people thought it beneficial to have two names.

Old Norse	Literal	English
Var þat þá átrúnaðr manna, at þeir menn myndi lengr lifa, sem tvau nöfn hefði.	Was that then believed men, to they men would longer live, which two names would-have.	It was then believed that men would live longer if they had two names.
Skjótt var þat auðsét á Helga, at hann myndi verða höfðingi mikill ok engi jafnaðarmaðr.	Soon was that easily-seen of Helga, to he would become chief great and no-one equal-man.	It was soon easily seen of Helgi that he would become a great chieftain and an unequal man.
Einn vetr lifði Þorsteinn hvíti, síðan þeir Þorsteinn fagri skilðu, ok þótti hann verit hafa it mesta mikil menni.	One winter lived Thorstein white, afterwards they Thorstein fair separated, and thought he been had the most great man.	Thorstein the White lived for one winter after Thorstein the Fair separated and he was thought to have been the greatest man.
Geitir í Krossavik átti Hallkötlu, dóttur Þiðranda ins gamla Ketilssonar þryms, sonar Geitis ok Hallkötlu.	Geitir in Krossavik married Hallkotla, daughter Thidrandi the old son-of-Ketil thrymr, son Geitis and Hallkotla.	Geitir of Krossavik married Hallkotla daughter of Thidrandi the old, son of Ketil Thunder, son of Geitir and Hallkotla.
Með þeim Geiti ok Brodd-Helga var vinátta mikil í fyrstu, en minnkað, svá sem á leið, ok varð ór fullr fjándskapr, sem segir í Vapnfirðinga sögu.	With them Geiti and Brodd-Helgi was friendship much at first, but lessened, so as it passed, and became from full fiendship, as said in Vopnafjord saga.	When them Geiti and Spike-Helgi was friendship much at first, but lessened as it passed, and became enmity as told in Vopnafjord saga.

Word List *(Old Norse to English)*

A, a

Old Norse	English
aðrir	others
af	from, of, off
afa	grandfather
afhenda	of-hand
afli	force
afsvör	of-answer
aftalði	of-told
aldri	age
alla	all
allan	all
allir	all
alllítilþægr	all-little-quiet
allra	all
allri	all
alls	all
allt	all
andaðist	died
andlát	death
annan	next
annarr	another
annars	another
annat	anything-else, other
aptr	again, back, return
arfs	inheritance
at	as, at, back-from, of, out, that, to
atferð	method
Atla	Atli (name)
Atlavik	Atlavik (place)
Atlavík	Atlavik (place)
auðigr	wealthy
auðsét	easily-seen
augnaverk	eye-injury
aust	eastern
austan	east
austmanni	eastern-man
austmenn	eastern-men
austr	east

Á, á

Old Norse	English
á	about, am, are, at, by, he, in, into, it, of, on, that, to
áðr	about, before
ákafa	zeal
Áslaug	Auslag (name)
ástir	love
Ásvaldsson	Son-of-Osvald (name)
Ásvarar	Asvar (name)
ásvör	Asvor (name)
átján	eighteen
átrúnaðr	believed
átta	eight
átti	had, married
áttu	had

Æ, æ

Old Norse	English
ætla	intended, suppose
ætlaði	intended
ætluðu	intended
ætta	had
ættar	noble

B, b

Old Norse	English
bað	asked, bid, proposed-to
báðir	both
báðu	bid
bæ	farm
bæði	both
bæta	compensate
bætir	compensate
bak	back
barna	born, children
barnæsku	childhood
batnaði	improved
bauð	invited, offered

Old Norse	English
beiddist	asked, to-ask
bellibragð	trick
bera	bear
bezt	best
beztr	best
bið	ask
bíða	wait
biði	asked
biðja	ask
biðr	asked, bid
bindr	tied
bjó	dwelt, lived, prepared
bjóða	bid
blindan	blind
boðit	invitation
Bolungarhöfn	Bolungarhof (place)
Bolungarvöllu	Bolungarvollu (place)
bónorðit	marriage-proposal, proposal
borinn	carried
borit	borne
börn	children
brá	startled
bráðgerr	quick
bræðr	brothers
bræðra	brothers
bræðrum	brothers
brðr	brothers
bregðir	action
brekkuna	slope
breytti	changed
brodda	shaft
Brodd-Helga	Brodd-Helgi (name)
Brodd-Helgi	Brodd-Helgi (name)
brú	bridge
brúðkaup	wedding
brúðkaupit	wedding
brúñkaupit	wedding
Brynjólfs	Brynolf's (name)
bta	compensate
bú	estate, farm
búi	estate
búigriðunginum	farm-bulls
búin	prepared
búinn	prepared
búinu	estate
búit	dwelling, lived
bundu	bound
búnir	prepared
burt	away
búsins	farm
byggðum	settlements
byrr	fair-wind

D, d

Old Norse	English
dætr	daughters
dag	day
daginn	day
dagverð	time-of-day-meal
dauða	death
dauðan	dead
dauðr	dead
dauðs	death
djúpa	deep
dó	died
dóttir	daughter
dóttur	daughter
drápu	killed
drengiliga	fellow-like
drengr	fellow
drepinn	killed
drepum	kill-we
duranna	the-door
durunum	door, the-door
dýrri	precious

E, e

Old Norse	English
ef	if
efniligr	promising
eggjaði	urged
eiga	owned
eigi	no, none, not
eigið	own
ein	alone
eina	one
Einar	Einar (name)
Einari	Einar (name)
einarr	Einar (name)

Old Norse	English
Einars	Einar's (name)
einn	alone, one
einskis	not
eitt	alone, one
ek	i
ekki	not
em	am
en	and, but, than
engan	none
engi	none, no-one
enn	one
ennit	head
eptir	after
er	as, be, if, is, that, was, when, which, who
ert	are
ertu	are-you
eru	are, were
eyðist	spending
eyðslumaðr	spending-man
eyru	ears
eyvindr	Eyvind (name)

F, f

Old Norse	English
fá	get
faðir	father
fætr	feet
fagra	fair, fair
fagri	fair
fái	get
fáir	few
fallinn	fallen
fallnir	fallen
fann	found
far	go
fár	unresponsive
fara	go, travel, travelled, went
farinn	travelling
farit	travel
farmannadaun	farmers-death
fastnaði	betrothed
fé	wealth
feðgar	father-and-son
féfátt	money-few
féit	fee
fekk	got, married
félag	company
félags	company
fell	fell
fellu	fell
fengit	caught
ferð	journey, travel
ferðinni	travelling
féþurfi	fee-needing
fimm	five, give
fimmta	five
finna	found
fjándliga	fiendishly
fjándskapr	fiendship
fjár	finances, wealth
fjárheimtingum	finances
fjárhlut	fee-lot, fee-lots
fjárhluti	possessions
fjárláninu	fee-loaning
fjárláns	fee-loan
fjarri	away
fjárskiptis	fee-exchange
flestum	most
flettir	Fleecer (name)
fljót	river
fljótinu	river
Fljótsdalsheiði	Fljotsdalsheidi (place)
Fljótsdalsheraði	Flotsdal-district (place)
flýti	hurry
flýtti	hurry
föður	father
föðurbróðir	father-brother
fór	travelled, went
fóru	travelled, went
förum	travel, travelling
förunautar	companions
fóst	foster
fóstra	foster, fosterer
fóstri	fosterer
frá	away, from
frænda	kinsman
frændi	cousin, kinsman

Old Norse	English
frændr	kinsmen
fram	from
framan	in-front-of
frásögn	from-saying
frði	took
frétti	heard
friðust	most-beautiful
frýði	persuaded
fullkominn	full-coming
fullr	full
fulltingi	assistance
fund	find, to-meet
fundar	meet
fundinn	found
fundust	found
fyrir	before, for
fyrr	before
fyrst	first
fyrstr	first
fyrstu	first

G, g

Old Norse	English
gabbaðir	mocked
gaf	gave
gáfu	gave
gakk	go
gamall	old
gamla	old
gamlan	old
ganga	go, going
gangast	go
gat	got
gaum	heed
gefa	give
gefit	given
gefizt	given
gefr	gave
gegnum	through
Geiti	Geiti (name)
Geitir	Geitir (name)
Geitis	Geitis (name)
gekk	going, went
geldr	paid
gengit	gone
gengr	went
gengu	went
gengust	went
ger	made
gera	do, done
gerast	will-be
gerði	did, gave, made
gerðist	became
gerðu	did
gerðust	made
geri	make
gerist	was
gert	done, made
gesti	guests
getit	told-of
gjalda	debt
glöggvastr	sharpest
góðan	good
góðar	good
góðir	good
goðorð	chieftain
góðr	good
Göngu-Hrólfssonar	Son-of-Gongu-Hrolf (name)
gott	good
góz	estate
gózi	belongings
græddi	profited
grafi	dig
grályndr	malicious
greiða	assistance
greiðliga	clearly
griðkona	the-house-keeper
griðkonuna	house-maiden
griðungarnir	bulls
griðungr	bull
gröf	ditch
gröfina	ditch
gröfinni	the-ditch
Guðrún	Gudrun (name)
gullhöttr	gold-hat
gullreknu	gold-plated

Old Norse	English

H, h

Old Norse	English
hætta	leave
haf	have
hafa	at-sea, had, have
hafði	had
hafi	had, sea
hag	benefit
hákonar	Hakon (name)
hald	hold
haldast	held
hálft	half-share
Hallkötlu	Hallkotla (name)
Hálogaland	Halogaland (place)
háls	hills
hálsi	neck
handa	hand
hann	he, him, his
hans	his
harðla	harden
hásetum	crew
haustit	autumn
hávaða	loud
hávaðamaðr	a-loud-man
heðan	from-here
hefði	would-have
hefi	have
hefir	had, has, have
heillavænligra	beneficial
heim	home
heima	home
heimagriðunginum	home-bull
heimagriðungrinn	home-bull, home-bulls
heimamaðr	home-man
heiman	home
heimtir	demanded
heimtu	demand
heiti	named
heitin	named
heitir	named
heitorði	title
heldr	held, rather
Helga	Helga (name)
Helgi	Helgi (name)
Helgu	Helga (name), Helga's (name)
helt	held
hendi	hand
hendr	hand, hands
hennar	her
hér	here
heraðit	district
herbergjum	rooms
herfiligan	harrowing-like
hesta	horses
hét	named, names
hétu	named
hingat	here
hinn	him
hitt	other
hitta	meet
hittir	met
hittu	met
hjá	beside
hlaði	farmyard
hlaupa	jump
hlaut	got
hleypr	ran
hljóp	ran
hlógu	laughed
hlotizt	lot
hlótt	laughed
hlut	share
hluti	things
Hnefilsdal	Hnefilsdal (place)
höfði	head
höfðingi	chief
höfðingja	chieftans
höfðu	had
hofi	Hof (place)
Hofland	Hofland (place)
Hofs	Hof (place)
Hofsmönnum	Men-of-Hof (place)
höfuð	head
höfum	have
Hofverja	of-Hof (place)
hol	hole
hon	she
hönd	hand
höndina	hand

Old Norse	English
honum	he, he, him, his
Hrafnssonar	Son-of-Hrafn (name)
Hrani	Hrani (name)
hrapa	hurried
Hróðgeirs	Hrodgeir (name)
hross	horses
hrossin	horses
hrumr	decrepit
hug	thoughts
hugar	mind
hugkvæmr	resourceful
hugmannliga	mentally
hugr	thought
hugsat	know
húsinu	of-the-house
húskarla	house-carls
húskarlar	house-carls
hvar	where
hvarf	disappeared
hvárratveggja	either-side
hvárt	either, whether
hvergi	nowhere
hverir	why
hverju	how
hvern	what
hverr	who
hvert	each
hví	why
hvíta	white
hvíti	white

I, i

Old Norse	English
illa	badly, ill
illt	ill
in	the
ina	the
Ingibjörg	Ingibjorg (name)
inn	in, the, then
inni	in, the
ins	the
it	the

Í, í

Old Norse	English
í	about, among, at, his, if, in, of, the, to, with
ílendust	landed
íslandi	Iceland (place)
íslands	Iceland (place)

J, j

Old Norse	English
jafnaðarmaðr	equally-man, equal-man
jafnan	equally
jafnræði	equally
jarls	earl
játar	accepts
jöfnum	equal
Jökulsá	Jokulsla (place)

K, k

Old Norse	English
kæmi	came
kalla	called
kallaðr	called
kallar	calls
karl	man
kaupbrigði	bargains
kaupir	bought
kaus	chose
kemr	came
kenndi	knew
Ketilssonar	Son-of-Ketil (name)
keypti	bought
kippti	snatched
klyfjar	hoof
klyfjum	hooves
kné	knee
koglaði	quivered
kom	came, comes
koma	came, come
komast	come
kominn	came, come, coming
komit	come, coming

Old Norse	English
komni	coming
komnir	came, coming
kómu	came
kona	wife, woman
konan	woman
konu	wife, woman
konuna	wife
kört	short
körtr	Kartur (name)
kostr	choice
Kraka	Kraki (name)
Krakadóttur	daughter-of-Kraka (name)
Kraki	Kraki (name)
Krossavik	Krossavik (place)
kumpánar	companions
kunna	knowing
kvað	said
kvaðst	said, spoke
kvánfang	wife
kvángaðr	married
kveða	sang
kveðr	said
kveðst	said
kvenna	woman, women
kvikfé	livestock

L, l

Old Norse	English
lá	laid, lay
laðaði	attracted
læk	brook
Lagarfljót	Lagarfljot (place)
lagði	laid, left
lagðist	lay
lagðr	laid
lán	loan
land	land
landi	land
landnámum	land-taking
langlífr	long-life
láta	leave, let
latti	discouraged
launa	repay
legg	lay
leggr	laid
leið	passed, way
leigðu	rented
leitaði	sought
lék	played
lendr	land
lengr	longer
let	let
lét	had, let
letja	let
létt	let
leystr	loosened
lézt	let
liðfárr	team-working
liði	company
liðinu	team
liðnum	passed
lifa	live
lifði	lived
líka	alike
líkast	like
lítil	little
litlu	little
lítt	little
lögðu	laid
lögðust	laid
lokit	ended
lönd	lands
lýkst	ended

M, m

Old Norse	English
má	may
maðr	man
mælti	said, spoke
mágr	brother-in-law
mágs	brother-in-law
mál	matter, matters
máli	matter, speak
máls	matter
málugr	talkative
mann	man, men
manna	men, people
mannanar	accomplishment
mannbroddarnir	spear

Old Norse	English
mannvænligir	men-promising
mannvænligsti	man-most-promising
marga	many
margbreytinn	many-varied
máttu	could
mátust	discussed
mdd	tired
með	with
meðallagi	middle-lying
meðan	long-as, with
meira	more
Melrakkasléttu	Melrakkasletta (place)
menn	men
menni	man
mér	me, my, to-me
mest	most
mesta	most
mesti	best
meta	appreciate
metnaðar	ambition
Miðfjörð	Midfjord (place)
mik	me
mikil	great, much
mikill	great, much
mikilli	much
mikinn	much
mikit	much
miklu	much
milli	between
millum	between
mín	for-me, mine, my
minn	mine
minni	less
minnkað	lessened
mínum	mine
missti	lost
mitt	mine
mjök	much
Möðrudalsheiði	Modrudalsheidi (place)
mönnum	men, people
morgins	morning
mun	shall, will
munda	would
mundu	should, would, would-be
muntu	shall
munu	shall
myndi	would

N, n

Old Norse	English
næsta	next
nætr	nights
nafna	namesake
nafni	namesake
nátt	night
naumudal	Naumudal (place)
naut	bulls
nautanna	bull
nefndist	named
nefndr	named
neitat	denied
nenna	care
niðr	down
nöfn	names
nökk	some
nökkur	some
nökkura	some
nökkut	some, somewhat
norðarliga	northerly
norðr	north
Nóreg	Norway (place)
nóregi	Norway (place)
Nóregs	Norway (place)
nú	not, now
numin	taken
nýkomin	newly-arrived, newly-come
nýtekit	newly-taken

O, o

Old Norse	English
of	of
ofan	above, down, over
ofráð	too-high
ofsamaðr	over-bearing-man
ok	and
okkar	ours
or	out-from

Old Norse	English
orð	word
orðsending	message
orðstír	reputation
orðum	words
Ormsár	Ormsa (place)
oss	us

Ó, ó

Old Norse	English
ódæll	unruly
ófriði	war
ógurligr	formidable
ólíkligr	unlikely
ór	from, out-from, out-of
Ósk	Osk (name)
óvæginn	ruthless
óvin	un-friend
óvíss	uncertain
óx	grew
óxu	grow

Ö, ö

Old Norse	English
öðrum	other
öll	all
öllu	all
öllum	all
Ölvir	Olvir (name)
Önundr	Onund (name)
Öxarfirði	Oxarfjord (place)
Öxna-Þórissonar	Son-of-Oxna-Thori (name)

P, p

Old Norse	English
prófa	prove

R, r

Old Norse	English
ráð	advice
ráðabreytni	decision-conduct
ráðahag	proposed
ráðahagsins	consult
ráði	advice
ráðir	advise
ráðizt	advise
ráðs	advice
ráðum	advice
ræðr	discussed
rammr	strong
rannsaka	search
réð	advised
réðst	decided
reið	rode
reiður	decided
reisir	raised
rekaströndum	rekastrondum
rekkjunnar	bed
Reyðarfjörð	Reydarfjord (place)
reyndist	turned-out
ríða	ride, rode
riðit	rode
ríðr	rode
risinn	risen
rit	considerable
röskr	strong
röskvasti	most-mature
rufu	tore
rúmi	room

S, s

Old Norse	English
sá	saw, so, the
sætt	settlement
sagði	said, said, told, told
sagðist	said
sagt	said, said
sakargiptir	sake-given
sakir	sake, sake-of
saman	together
samferðir	interaction
sanna	truth
sannligt	true-like
satt	truth
sauðhús	sheep-house
segði	said
segi	said

Word List (Old Norse to English)

Old Norse	English
segir	said, say, told
segist	said
segja	say, tell, to-say
seinkaði	delayed
sekr	guilty
sel	sell
seldi	sold
selinu	shed
selit	shed
sels	shed
selsdurunum	shed-door
selt	sold
selvegginum	shed-ways
sem	as, was, which
sér	as, he, him, himself, his, saw, that, themselves, this, with
sérliga	especially
setja	sit
sett	set
síðan	after, afterwards, since
síðar	afterwards
síðr	less
síðustu	finally
Sigurðr	Sigurd (name)
sik	himself
sína	his, theirs
sinn	his, that
sinni	his
síns	his
sínu	his, theirs
sínum	his, theirs
sitt	his
sjálfdmi	self-example
sjálfr	himself
sjau	seven
sjóði	funds
sjónina	sight
skaði	loss
skálagerðar	hut-make
skalt	shall
skamma	short
skapi	mood
skaplyndi	mind, temper, temperament

Old Norse	English
skaplyndis	temper
skapraun	temperament
Skeggjastöðum	Skeggjastadir (place)
skemmsta	shortest
skemmu	storehouse
skemmuna	sleeping-room
skikkju	cloak
skilðim	parted
skilðu	separated
skiljast	separated
skip	ship, ships
skipi	ship
skipit	ship
skipmenn	ship-men
skips	ship, ships
skipsöluna	ship's-sale
skipta	divided
skipti	changed
skir	fetched
skja	seek
skjöldinn	shield
skjótt	quickly, soon
skóg	forest
skóm	shoes
skuld	should
skuldalið	indebted
skuldanautrinn	debtor
skuldastaðrinn	debt
skuluð	should
skyldi	should, would
skyldu	should, would
skylt	should
skyrbjúg	scurvy
slá	struck
slíkt	such
Smjörvatnsheiði	Smjorvatnsheidi (place)
smst	same
snarar	sneaked
snemma	early
sneri	turned
sneypu	shame
sögu	saga
sögunni	the-saga
sömu	same
son	son

Old Norse	English
sonar	son, son's
sonr	son, son-of
sonu	sons
sótt	sickness
sóttir	sought
sóttu	sought
spjót	spear
spjóti	spear
spjótinu	spear
spjótit	spear
spottar	mocked
sprettr	sprang
spurði	asked
spurðr	asked
spurðust	learned-of
stað	place
staðar	place
staddr	standing
standa	stand
stangar	stabbed
stangast	stabbed
steinbirni	Steinbjorn (name), Steinbjorn's (name)
steinbjarnar	Steinbjorn (name)
steinbjörn	Steinbjorn (name)
sterkr	strong
stóð	stood
stoða	stood
stöðli	standing
stökk	fled
stönguðust	stabbing
stóra	great
stórmannligr	great-man-like
stórr	great, large
stund	awhile, while
stundar	awhile
sumar	summer
sumarit	summer
sumri	summer
sumur	summers
svá	so
svaraði	answered
svarar	answered
svefns	sleep
svefnskemmunnar	sleeping-room
sveinninn	boy
Sveinungsvík	Sveinungsvik (place)
sveitarhöfðingi	rural-chief
svivirði	dishonoured
svör	answer
synir	sons
synja	refuse

T, t

Old Norse	English
tæki	take
taka	take, took
takast	take
tekr	take, took
telr	counted
tíðenda	news
tíðendi	news, tidings
tíðendin	news
tíðendum	news
til	for, to, until
tillag	proposal
tillaga	proposal
tilsögu	to-say
tímum	time
tók	took
tókust	took
Tóptavelli	Toftavellir (place)
trúa	trusted
trúið	trust
tuttugu	twenty
tvá	two
tvau	two
tveir	two

Þ, þ

Old Norse	English
þá	then
þaðan	from-there
þangat	from-there
þann	he, that
þar	then, there
þat	it, that
þau	the, then, they
þegar	already, straight-away, then, when

Old Norse	English
þeim	that, the, them, they
þeir	they
þeira	of-them, their, theirs
þeirar	their, there
þér	to-you, you, your
þess	this
þessa	this
þessari	this
þessu	this
þetta	that, the, this
Þiðranda	Thidrandi (name)
þiggja	accept, receive
þik	you
þín	you
þinn	yours
þinni	yours
þíns	yours
þínum	your, yours
Þistilsfjarðar	Thistilsfjord (place)
þitt	yours
þó	though
Þóra	Thora (name)
Þorbjarnar	Thorbjorn (name), Thorbjorn's (name)
Þorbjörg	Thorbjorg (name)
Þorbjörn	Thorbjorn (name)
Þórðr	Thord (name)
Þorfinnr	Thorfin (name)
Þorfinns	Thorfin's (name)
Þorfinnsson	Son-of-Thorfin (name)
Þorfinnssyni	son-of-Thorfin (name)
Þorgerðr	Thorgerd (name)
Þorgils	Thorgils (name)
Þorgilsi	Thorgils's (name)
Þorgilsson	Son-of-Thorgils (name)
Þóri	Thori (name)
Þórir	Thori (name)
Þóris	Thorir (name)
Þórisdóttur	Daughter-of-Thorri (name)
Þórisson	Son-of-Thorri (name)
Þorkell	Thorkell (name)
Þorstein	Thorstein (name)
Þorsteini	Thorstein (name)
Þorsteinn	Thorstein (name)

Old Norse	English
Þorsteins	Son-of-Thorstein (name), Thorstein's (name)
þorum	dare
þótti	seemed, thought, thought-of
þóttist	thought
þóttust	thought
þrévetr	three-winters
þriði	third
þriðji	third
þrítugr	thirty
þrjá	three
þryms	thrymr
þú	you
þungt	unhappy
þurfa	needed
þurftu	needed
því	because, for, since, that, then, therefore
þykkir	considered, seemed, think
þykkist	seemed
þykkja	thought

U, u

ullhött	woolen-hat
um	about
umsýslu	administered, administration, administrations
undan	away, away-from, under
unga	young
unz	until
upp	up
upphafsmaðr	instigator
uppi	up
urðu	became

Ú, ú

út	back, out
útan	out, out-of

Old Norse	English
útanferðar	out-travel
úti	about, outside

V, v

Old Norse	English
vænn	kind
vænst	fair
væri	was, were, would-be
vakti	awoke
vánbiðill	hopeful
vanda	problems
vanfærr	disabled
vanhluta	part
vápna	Vopnafjord (place)
vápnafirði	Vopnafjord (place)
Vápnafjarðar	Vopnafjord (place)
vápnafjörð	Vopnafjord (place)
Vapnfirðinga	Vopnafjord (place)
var	was
vár	spring
varð	became, was
várit	spring
váru	ours, was, were
vaskasti	boldest
vaskligr	diligent
vatn	water
váttar	witnesses
veg	way
vegginum	roof
veit	know
veitti	grant
veitts	bestowing
vek	wake
vekja	awoke
vel	well
ver	be
vér	we
vera	be, been, had-been
verða	be, become
verðr	became, bring
verit	be, became, been, made
versna	worst
vestr	west
vestrdalsár	Vesturdalsa (place)
vesuðust	felt
vetr	winter, winters
vetra	winters
vetrhúsum	winter-house
vetrinn	winter
við	therefore, with
viðrnefni	nickname
viðum	wood
vig	killing
víg	killing
vil	will, wish
vilda	will
vildi	willed, wished
vilja	will, willed
viljum	will
vill	will
villt	will
villtu	will-you
vinátta	friendship
vináttu	friendship
vinr	friend
vinsælastr	popular
vinsæll	popularity
vinsælust	popular
vinveittr	friendly
virði	valued
virðingar	worthiness
virðist	seems
virðr	respect
viss	know
víss	surely
vissi	knew
víst	certainly
vit	with
vita	knew, know
vitat	know
vitrliga	wise-like
vörðust	guarded
vöru	wares

Y, y

Old Norse	English
yfir	across, over
yrði	would
Yrjar	Yrjar (place)

Word List *(English to Old Norse)*

A, a

English	Old Norse
about	*á, áðr, í, um, úti*
above	*ofan*
accept	*þiggja*
accepts	*játar*
accomplishment	*mannanar*
across	*yfir*
action	*bregðir*
administered	*umsýslu*
administration	*umsýslu*
administrations	*umsýslu*
advice	*ráð, ráði, ráðs, ráðum*
advise	*ráðir, ráðizt*
advised	*réð*
after	*eptir, síðan*
afterwards	*síðan, síðar*
again	*aptr*
age	*aldri*
alike	*líka*
all	*alla, allan, allir, allra, allri, alls, allt, öll, öllu, öllum*
all-little-quiet	*alllítilþægr*
alone	*ein, einn, eitt*
a-loud-man	*háváðamaðr*
already	*þegar*
am	*á, em*
ambition	*metnaðar*
among	*í*
and	*en, ok*
another	*annarr, annars*
answer	*svör*
answered	*svaraði, svarar*
anything-else	*annat*
appreciate	*meta*
are	*á, ert, eru*
are-you	*ertu*
as	*at, er, sem, sér*
ask	*bið, biðja*
asked	*bað, beiddist, biði, biðr, spurði, spurðr*
assistance	*fulltingi, greiða*
Asvar (name)	*Ásvarar*
Asvor (name)	*ásvör*
at	*á, at, í*
Atlavik (place)	*Atlavik, Atlavík*
Atli (name)	*Atla*
at-sea	*hafa*
attracted	*laðaði*
Auslag (name)	*Áslaug*
autumn	*haustit*
away	*burt, fjarri, frá, undan*
away-from	*undan*
awhile	*stund, stundar*
awoke	*vakti, vekja*

B, b

English	Old Norse
back	*aptr, bak, út*
back-from	*at*
badly	*illa*
bargains	*kaupbrigði*
be	*er, ver, vera, verða, verit*
bear	*bera*
became	*gerðist, urðu, varð, verðr, verit*
because	*því*
become	*verða*
bed	*rekkjunnar*
been	*vera, verit*
before	*áðr, fyrir, fyrr*
believed	*átrúnaðr*
belongings	*gózi*
beneficial	*heillavænligra*
benefit	*hag*
beside	*hjá*
best	*bezt, beztr, mesti*
bestowing	*veitts*
betrothed	*fastnaði*
between	*milli, millum*
bid	*bað, báðu, biðr, bjóða*
blind	*blindan*

English	*Old Norse*
boldest	*vaskasti*
Bolungarhof (place)	*Bolungarhöfn*
Bolungarvollu (place)	*Bolungarvöllu*
born	*barna*
borne	*borit*
both	*báðir, bæði*
bought	*kaupir, keypti*
bound	*bundu*
boy	*sveinninn*
bridge	*brú*
bring	*verðr*
Brodd-Helgi (name)	*Brodd-Helga, Brodd-Helgi*
brook	*læk*
brother-in-law	*mágr, mágs*
brothers	*bræðr, bræðra, bræðrum, brðr*
Brynolf's (name)	*Brynjólfs*
bull	*griðungr, nautanna*
bulls	*griðungarnir, naut*
but	*en*
by	*á*

C, c

English	*Old Norse*
called	*kalla, kallaðr*
calls	*kallar*
came	*kæmi, kemr, kom, koma, kominn, komnir, kómu*
care	*nenna*
carried	*borinn*
caught	*fengit*
certainly	*víst*
changed	*breytti, skipti*
chief	*höfðingi*
chieftain	*goðorð*
chieftans	*höfðingja*
childhood	*barnæsku*
children	*barna, börn*
choice	*kostr*
chose	*kaus*
clearly	*greiðliga*
cloak	*skikkju*
come	*koma, komast, kominn, komit*
comes	*kom*
coming	*kominn, komit, komni, komnir*
companions	*förunautar, kumpánar*
company	*félag, félags, liði*
compensate	*bæta, bætir, bta*
considerable	*rit*
considered	*þykkir*
consult	*ráðahagsins*
could	*máttu*
counted	*telr*
cousin	*frændi*
crew	*hásetum*

D, d

English	*Old Norse*
dare	*þorum*
daughter	*dóttir, dóttur*
daughter-of-Kraka (name)	*Krakadóttur*
Daughter-of-Thorri (name)	*Þórisdóttur*
daughters	*dætr*
day	*dag, daginn*
dead	*dauðan, dauðr*
death	*andlát, dauða, dauðs*
debt	*gjalda, skuldastaðrinn*
debtor	*skuldanautrinn*
decided	*réðst, reiður*
decision-conduct	*ráðabreytni*
decrepit	*hrumr*
deep	*djúpa*
delayed	*seinkaði*
demand	*heimtu*
demanded	*heimtir*
denied	*neitat*
did	*gerði, gerðu*
died	*andaðist, dó*
dig	*grafi*
diligent	*vaskligr*
disabled	*vanfærr*
disappeared	*hvarf*
discouraged	*latti*

English	Old Norse
discussed	*mátust, ræðr*
dishonoured	*svivirði*
district	*heraðit*
ditch	*gröf, gröfina*
divided	*skipta*
do	*gera*
done	*gera, gert*
door	*durunum*
down	*niðr, ofan*
dwelling	*búit*
dwelt	*bjó*

E, e

English	Old Norse
each	*hvert*
earl	*jarls*
early	*snemma*
ears	*eyru*
easily-seen	*auðsét*
east	*austan, austr*
eastern	*aust*
eastern-man	*austmanni*
eastern-men	*austmenn*
eight	*átta*
eighteen	*átján*
Einar (name)	*Einar, Einari, einarr*
Einar's (name)	*Einars*
either	*hvárt*
either-side	*hvárratveggja*
ended	*lokit, lýkst*
equal	*jöfnum*
equally	*jafnan, jafnræði*
equally-man	*jafnaðarmaðr*
equal-man	*jafnaðarmaðr*
especially	*sérliga*
estate	*bú, búi, búinu, góz*
eye-injury	*augnaverk*
Eyvind (name)	*eyvindr*

F, f

English	Old Norse
fair	*fagra, fagri, vænst*
fair-wind	*byrr*
fallen	*fallinn, fallnir*
farm	*bæ, bú, búsins*
farm-bulls	*búigriðunginum*
farmers-death	*farmannadaun*
farmyard	*hlaði*
father	*faðir, föður*
father-and-son	*feðgar*
father-brother	*föðurbróðir*
fee	*féit*
fee-exchange	*fjárskiptis*
fee-loan	*fjárláns*
fee-loaning	*fjárláninu*
fee-lot	*fjárhlut*
fee-lots	*fjárhlut*
fee-needing	*féþurfi*
feet	*fætr*
fell	*fell, fellu*
fellow	*drengr*
fellow-like	*drengiliga*
felt	*vesuðust*
fetched	*skir*
few	*fáir*
fiendishly	*fjándliga*
fiendship	*fjándskapr*
finally	*síðustu*
finances	*fjár, fjárheimtingum*
find	*fund*
first	*fyrst, fyrstr, fyrstu*
five	*fimm, fimmta*
fled	*stökk*
Fleecer (name)	*flettir*
Fljotsdalsheidi (place)	*Fljótsdalsheiði*
Flotsdal-district (place)	*Fljótsdalsheraði*
for	*fyrir, því, til*
force	*afli*
forest	*skóg*
for-me	*mín*
formidable	*ógurligr*
foster	*fóst, fóstra*
fosterer	*fóstra, fóstri*
found	*fann, finna, fundinn, fundust*
friend	*vinr*
friendly	*vinveittr*
friendship	*vinátta, vináttu*
from	*af, frá, fram, ór*

English	Old Norse
from-here	*heðan*
from-saying	*frásögn*
from-there	*þaðan, þangat*
full	*fullr*
full-coming	*fullkominn*
funds	*sjóði*

G, g

English	Old Norse
gave	*gaf, gáfu, gefr, gerði*
Geiti (name)	*Geiti*
Geitir (name)	*Geitir*
Geitis (name)	*Geitis*
get	*fá, fái*
give	*fimm, gefa*
given	*gefit, gefizt*
go	*far, fara, gakk, ganga, gangast*
going	*ganga, gekk*
gold-hat	*gullhöttr*
gold-plated	*gullreknu*
gone	*gengit*
good	*góðan, góðar, góðir, góðr, gott*
got	*fekk, gat, hlaut*
grandfather	*afa*
grant	*veitti*
great	*mikil, mikill, stóra, stórr*
great-man-like	*stórmannligr*
grew	*óx*
grow	*óxu*
guarded	*vörðust*
Gudrun (name)	*Guðrún*
guests	*gesti*
guilty	*sekr*

H, h

English	Old Norse
had	*ætta, átti, áttu, hafa, hafði, hafi, hefir, höfðu, lét*
had-been	*vera*
Hakon (name)	*hákonar*
half-share	*hálft*
Hallkotla (name)	*Hallkötlu*
Halogaland (place)	*Hálogaland*
hand	*handa, hendi, hendr, hönd, höndina*
hands	*hendr*
harden	*harðla*
harrowing-like	*herfiligan*
has	*hefir*
have	*haf, hafa, hefi, hefir, höfum*
he	*á, hann, honum, sér, þann*
head	*ennit, höfði, höfuð*
heard	*frétti*
heed	*gaum*
held	*haldast, heldr, helt*
Helga (name)	*Helga, Helgu*
Helga's (name)	*Helgu*
Helgi (name)	*Helgi*
her	*hennar*
here	*hér, hingat*
hills	*háls*
him	*hann, hinn, honum, sér*
himself	*sér, sik, sjálfr*
his	*hann, hans, honum, í, sér, sína, sinn, sinni, síns, sínu, sínum, sitt*
Hnefilsdal (place)	*Hnefilsdal*
Hof (place)	*hofi, Hofs*
Hofland (place)	*Hofland*
hold	*hald*
hole	*hol*
home	*heim, heima, heiman*
home-bull	*heimagriðunginum, heimagriðungrinn*
home-bulls	*heimagriðungrinn*
home-man	*heimamaðr*
hoof	*klyfjar*
hooves	*klyfjum*
hopeful	*vánbiðill*
horses	*hesta, hross, hrossin*
house-carls	*húskarla, húskarlar*
house-maiden	*griðkonuna*
how	*hverju*
Hrani (name)	*Hrani*
Hrodgeir (name)	*Hróðgeirs*

English	*Old Norse*
hurried	*hrapa*
hurry	*flýti, flýtti*
hut-make	*skálagerðar*

I, i

English	*Old Norse*
i	*ek*
Iceland (place)	*íslandi, íslands*
if	*ef, er, í*
ill	*illa, illt*
improved	*batnaði*
in	*á, í, inn, inni*
indebted	*skuldalið*
in-front-of	*framan*
Ingibjorg (name)	*Ingibjörg*
inheritance	*arfs*
instigator	*upphafsmaðr*
intended	*ætla, ætlaði, ætluðu*
interaction	*samferðir*
into	*á*
invitation	*boðit*
invited	*bauð*
is	*er*
it	*á, þat*

J, j

English	*Old Norse*
Jokulsla (place)	*Jökulsá*
journey	*ferð*
jump	*hlaupa*

K, k

English	*Old Norse*
Kartur (name)	*körtr*
killed	*drápu, drepinn*
killing	*vig, víg*
kill-we	*drepum*
kind	*vænn*
kinsman	*frænda, frændi*
kinsmen	*frændr*
knee	*kné*
knew	*kenndi, vissi, vita*
know	*hugsat, veit, viss, vita, vitat*
knowing	*kunna*
Kraki (name)	*Kraka, Kraki*
Krossavik (place)	*Krossavik*

L, l

English	*Old Norse*
Lagarfljot (place)	*Lagarfljót*
laid	*lá, lagði, lagðr, leggr, lögðu, lögðust*
land	*land, landi, lendr*
landed	*ílendust*
lands	*lönd*
land-taking	*landnámum*
large	*stórr*
laughed	*hlógu, hlótt*
lay	*lá, lagðist, legg*
learned-of	*spurðust*
leave	*hætta, láta*
left	*lagði*
less	*minni, síðr*
lessened	*minnkað*
let	*láta, let, lét, letja, létt, lézt*
like	*líkast*
little	*lítil, litlu, lítt*
live	*lifa*
lived	*bjó, búit, lifði*
livestock	*kvikfé*
loan	*lán*
long-as	*meðan*
longer	*lengr*
long-life	*langlífr*
loosened	*leystr*
loss	*skaði*
lost	*missti*
lot	*hlotizt*
loud	*hávaða*
love	*ástir*

M, m

English	*Old Norse*
made	*ger, gerði, gerðust, gert, verit*

English	Old Norse
make	*geri*
malicious	*grályndr*
man	*karl, maðr, mann, menni*
man-most-promising	*mannvænligsti*
many	*marga*
many-varied	*margbreytinn*
marriage-proposal	*bónorðit*
married	*átti, fekk, kvángaðr*
matter	*mál, máli, máls*
matters	*mál*
may	*má*
me	*mér, mik*
meet	*fundar, hitta*
Melrakkasletta (place)	*Melrakkasléttu*
men	*mann, manna, menn, mönnum*
Men-of-Hof (place)	*Hofsmönnum*
men-promising	*mannvænligir*
mentally	*hugmannliga*
message	*orðsending*
met	*hittir, hittu*
method	*atferð*
middle-lying	*meðallagi*
Midfjord (place)	*Miðfjörð*
mind	*hugar, skaplyndi*
mine	*mín, minn, mínum, mitt*
mocked	*gabbaðir, spottar*
Modrudalsheidi (place)	*Möðrudalsheiði*
money-few	*féfátt*
mood	*skapi*
more	*meira*
morning	*morgins*
most	*flestum, mest, mesta*
most-beautiful	*friðust*
most-mature	*röskvasti*
much	*mikil, mikill, mikilli, mikinn, mikit, miklu, mjök*
my	*mér, mín*

N, n

English	Old Norse
named	*heiti, heitin, heitir, hét, hétu, nefndist, nefndr*
names	*hét, nöfn*
namesake	*nafna, nafni*
Naumudal (place)	*naumudal*
neck	*hálsi*
needed	*þurfa, þurftu*
newly-arrived	*nýkomin*
newly-come	*nýkomin*
newly-taken	*nýtekit*
news	*tíðenda, tíðendi, tíðendin, tíðendum*
next	*annan, næsta*
nickname	*viðrnefni*
night	*nátt*
nights	*nætr*
no	*eigi*
noble	*ættar*
none	*eigi, engan, engi*
no-one	*engi*
north	*norðr*
northerly	*norðarliga*
Norway (place)	*Nóreg, nóregi, Nóregs*
not	*eigi, einskis, ekki, nú*
now	*nú*
nowhere	*hvergi*

O, o

English	Old Norse
of	*á, af, at, í, of*
of-answer	*afsvör*
off	*af*
offered	*bauð*
of-hand	*afhenda*
of-Hof (place)	*Hofverja*
of-the-house	*húsinu*
of-them	*þeira*
of-told	*aftalði*
old	*gamall, gamla, gamlan*
Olvir (name)	*Ölvir*
on	*á*
one	*eina, einn, eitt, enn*
Onund (name)	*Önundr*
Ormsa (place)	*Ormsár*

English	*Old Norse*
Osk (name)	*Ósk*
other	*annat, hitt, öðrum*
others	*aðrir*
ours	*okkar, váru*
out	*at, út, útan*
out-from	*or, ór*
out-of	*ór, útan*
outside	*úti*
out-travel	*útanferðar*
over	*ofan, yfir*
over-bearing-man	*ofsamaðr*
own	*eigið*
owned	*eiga*
Oxarfjord (place)	*Öxarfirði*

P, p

English	*Old Norse*
paid	*geldr*
part	*vanhluta*
parted	*skilðim*
passed	*leið, liðnum*
people	*manna, mönnum*
persuaded	*frýði*
place	*stað, staðar*
played	*lék*
popular	*vinsælastr, vinsælust*
popularity	*vinsæll*
possessions	*fjárhluti*
precious	*dýrri*
prepared	*bjó, búin, búinn, búnir*
problems	*vanda*
profited	*græddi*
promising	*efniligr*
proposal	*bónorðit, tillag, tillaga*
proposed	*ráðahag*
proposed-to	*bað*
prove	*prófa*

Q, q

English	*Old Norse*
quick	*bráðgerr*
quickly	*skjótt*
quivered	*koglaði*

R, r

English	*Old Norse*
raised	*reisir*
ran	*hleypr, hljóp*
rather	*heldr*
receive	*þiggja*
refuse	*synja*
rekastrondum	*rekaströndum*
rented	*leigðu*
repay	*launa*
reputation	*orðstír*
resourceful	*hugkvæmr*
respect	*virðr*
return	*aptr*
Reydarfjord (place)	*Reyðarfjörð*
ride	*ríða*
risen	*risinn*
river	*fljót, fljótinu*
rode	*reið, ríða, riðit, ríðr*
roof	*vegginum*
room	*rúmi*
rooms	*herbergjum*
rural-chief	*sveitarhöfðingi*
ruthless	*óvæginn*

S, s

English	*Old Norse*
saga	*sögu*
said	*kvað, kvaðst, kveðr, kveðst, mælti, sagði, sagðist, sagt, segði, segi, segir, segist*
sake	*sakir*
sake-given	*sakargiptir*
sake-of	*sakir*
same	*smst, sömu*
sang	*kveða*
saw	*sá, sér*
say	*segir, segja*
scurvy	*skyrbjúg*
sea	*hafi*
search	*rannsaka*
seek	*skja*
seemed	*þótti, þykkir, þykkist*

English	Old Norse
seems	*virðist*
self-example	*sjálfdmi*
sell	*sel*
separated	*skilðu, skiljast*
set	*sett*
settlement	*sætt*
settlements	*byggðum*
seven	*sjau*
shaft	*brodda*
shall	*mun, muntu, munu, skalt*
shame	*sneypu*
share	*hlut*
sharpest	*glöggvastr*
she	*hon*
shed	*selinu, selit, sels*
shed-door	*selsdurunum*
shed-ways	*selvegginum*
sheep-house	*sauðhús*
shield	*skjöldinn*
ship	*skip, skipi, skipit, skips*
ship-men	*skipmenn*
ships	*skip, skips*
ship's-sale	*skipsöluna*
shoes	*skóm*
short	*kört, skamma*
shortest	*skemmsta*
should	*mundu, skuld, skuluð, skyldi, skyldu, skylt*
sickness	*sótt*
sight	*sjónina*
Sigurd (name)	*Sigurðr*
since	*síðan, því*
sit	*setja*
Skeggjastadir (place)	*Skeggjastöðum*
sleep	*svefns*
sleeping-room	*skemmuna, svefnskemmunnar*
slope	*brekkuna*
Smjorvatnsheidi (place)	*Smjörvatnsheiði*
snatched	*kippti*
sneaked	*snarar*
so	*sá, svá*
sold	*seldi, selt*

English	Old Norse
some	*nökk, nökkur, nökkura, nökkut*
somewhat	*nökkut*
son	*son, sonar, sonr*
son-of	*sonr*
Son-of-Gongu-Hrolf (name)	*Göngu-Hrólfssonar*
Son-of-Hrafn (name)	*Hrafnssonar*
Son-of-Ketil (name)	*Ketilssonar*
Son-of-Osvald (name)	*Ásvaldsson*
Son-of-Oxna-Thori (name)	*Öxna-Þórissonar*
Son-of-Thorfin (name)	*Þorfinnsson, Þorfinnssyni*
Son-of-Thorgils (name)	*Þorgilsson*
Son-of-Thorri (name)	*Þórisson*
Son-of-Thorstein (name)	*Þorsteins*
sons	*sonu, synir*
son's	*sonar*
soon	*skjótt*
sought	*leitaði, sóttir, sóttu*
speak	*máli*
spear	*mannbroddarnir, spjót, spjóti, spjótinu, spjótit*
spending	*eyðist*
spending-man	*eyðslumaðr*
spoke	*kvaðst, mælti*
sprang	*sprettr*
spring	*vár, várit*
stabbed	*stangar, stangast*
stabbing	*stönguðust*
stand	*standa*
standing	*staddr, stöðli*
startled	*brá*
Steinbjorn (name)	*steinbirni, steinbjarnar, steinbjörn*
Steinbjorn's (name)	*steinbirni*
stood	*stóð, stoða*
storehouse	*skemmu*
straight-away	*þegar*
strong	*rammr, röskr, sterkr*
struck	*slá*
such	*slíkt*

English	*Old Norse*
summer	*sumar, sumarit, sumri*
summers	*sumur*
suppose	*ætla*
surely	*víss*
Sveinungsvik (place)	*Sveinungsvík*

T, t

English	*Old Norse*
take	*tæki, taka, takast, tekr*
taken	*numin*
talkative	*málugr*
team	*liðinu*
team-working	*liðfárr*
tell	*segja*
temper	*skaplyndi, skaplyndis*
temperament	*skaplyndi, skapraun*
than	*en*
that	*á, at, er, sér, sinn, þann, þat, þeim, þetta, því*
the	*í, in, ina, inn, inni, ins, it, sá, þau, þeim, þetta*
the-ditch	*gröfinni*
the-door	*duranna, durunum*
the-house-keeper	*griðkona*
their	*þeira, þeirar*
theirs	*sína, sínu, sínum, þeira*
them	*þeim*
themselves	*sér*
then	*inn, þá, þar, þau, þegar, því*
there	*þar, þeirar*
therefore	*því, við*
the-saga	*sögunni*
they	*þau, þeim, þeir*
Thidrandi (name)	*Þiðranda*
things	*hluti*
think	*þykkir*
third	*þriði, þriðji*
thirty	*þrítugr*
this	*sér, þess, þessa, þessari, þessu, þetta*
Thistilsfjord (place)	*Þistilsfjarðar*
Thora (name)	*Þóra*
Thorbjorg (name)	*Þorbjörg*
Thorbjorn (name)	*Þorbjarnar, Þorbjörn*
Thorbjorn's (name)	*Þorbjarnar*
Thord (name)	*Þórðr*
Thorfin (name)	*Þorfinnr*
Thorfin's (name)	*Þorfinns*
Thorgerd (name)	*Þorgerðr*
Thorgils (name)	*Þorgils*
Thorgils's (name)	*Þorgilsi*
Thori (name)	*Þóri, Þórir*
Thorir (name)	*Þóris*
Thorkell (name)	*Þorkell*
Thorstein (name)	*Þorstein, Þorsteini, Þorsteinn*
Thorstein's (name)	*Þorsteins*
though	*þó*
thought	*hugr, þótti, þóttist, þóttust, þykkja*
thought-of	*þótti*
thoughts	*hug*
three	*þrjá*
three-winters	*þrévetr*
through	*gegnum*
thrymr	*þryms*
tidings	*tíðendi*
tied	*bindr*
time	*tímum*
time-of-day-meal	*dagverð*
tired	*mdd*
title	*heitorði*
to	*á, at, í, til*
to-ask	*beiddist*
Toftavellir (place)	*Tóptavelli*
together	*saman*
told	*sagði, segir*
told-of	*getit*
to-me	*mér*
to-meet	*fund*
too-high	*ofráð*
took	*frði, taka, tekr, tók, tókust*
tore	*rufu*
to-say	*segja, tilsögu*
to-you	*þér*
travel	*fara, farit, ferð, förum*
travelled	*fara, fór, fóru*
travelling	*farinn, ferðinni, förum*

English	Old Norse
trick	*bellibragð*
true-like	*sannligt*
trust	*trúið*
trusted	*trúa*
truth	*sanna, satt*
turned	*sneri*
turned-out	*reyndist*
twenty	*tuttugu*
two	*tvá, tvau, tveir*

U, u

English	Old Norse
uncertain	*óvíss*
under	*undan*
un-friend	*óvin*
unhappy	*þungt*
unlikely	*ólíkligr*
unresponsive	*fár*
unruly	*ódæll*
until	*til, unz*
up	*upp, uppi*
urged	*eggjaði*
us	*oss*

V, v

English	Old Norse
valued	*virði*
Vesturdalsa (place)	*vestrdalsár*
Vopnafjord (place)	*vápna, vápnafirði, Vápnafjarðar, vápnafjörð, Vapnfirðinga*

W, w

English	Old Norse
wait	*bíða*
wake	*vek*
war	*ófriði*
wares	*vöru*
was	*er, gerist, sem, væri, var, varð, váru*
water	*vatn*
way	*leið, veg*
we	*vér*
wealth	*fé, fjár*
wealthy	*auðigr*
wedding	*brúðkaup, brúðkaupit, brúñkaupit*
well	*vel*
went	*fara, fór, fóru, gekk, gengr, gengu, gengust*
were	*eru, væri, váru*
west	*vestr*
what	*hvern*
when	*er, þegar*
where	*hvar*
whether	*hvárt*
which	*er, sem*
while	*stund*
white	*hvíta, hvíti*
who	*er, hverr*
why	*hverir, hví*
wife	*kona, konu, konuna, kvánfang*
will	*mun, vil, vilda, vilja, viljum, vill, villt*
will-be	*gerast*
willed	*vildi, vilja*
will-you	*villtu*
winter	*vetr, vetrinn*
winter-house	*vetrhúsum*
winters	*vetr, vetra*
wise-like	*vitrliga*
wish	*vil*
wished	*vildi*
with	*í, með, meðan, sér, við, vit*
witnesses	*váttar*
woman	*kona, konan, konu, kvenna*
women	*kvenna*
wood	*viðum*
woolen-hat	*ullhött*
word	*orð*
words	*orðum*
worst	*versna*
worthiness	*virðingar*
would	*munda, mundu, myndi, skyldi, skyldu, yrði*

English	*Old Norse*
would-be	*mundu, væri*
would-have	*hefði*

Y, y

English	*Old Norse*
you	*þér, þik, þín, þú*
young	*unga*
your	*þér, þínum*
yours	*þinn, þinni, þíns, þínum, þitt*
Yrjar (place)	*Yrjar*

The Saga of Thorstein the White (*Old Icelandic*)

Old Icelandic	Literal	English
1	**1**	**1**
Maður hét Ölvir hinn hvíti.	Man named Olvir the white.	There was a man named Olvir the White.
Hann var Ósvaldsson, Göngu-Hrólfssonar, Öxna-Þórissonar.	He was son-of-Osvald, son-of-Gongu-Hrolf, son-of-Oxna-Thori.	He was the son of Osvald, son of Gongu-Hrolf, son of Oxna-Thori.
Hann var lendur maður í Noregi og bjó í Naumudal.	He was land man of Norway and lived in Naumudal.	He was a landed man of Norway and lived in Naumudal.
Hann stökk fyrir ófriði Hákonar jarls á Yrjar og dó þar.	He fled before war Hakon earl on Yrjar and died there.	He fled before the war with earl Hakon on Yrjar and died there.
Hann átti einn son barna er Þorsteinn hét og var kallaður Þorsteinn hvíti.	He had one son born was Thorstein named and was called Thorstein white.	He had one son born who was named Thorstein and was called Thorstein the White.
Hann fór þegar eftir andlát föður síns út til Íslands með alla fjárhluti sína og kom skipi sínu í Vopnafjörð.	He travelled straight-away after death father his out to Iceland with all possessions his and came ship his to Vopnafjord.	He travelled straight-away after the death of his father out to Iceland with all his possessions and his ship came to Vopnafjord.
En þá var lokið landnámum á öllu Íslandi.	But then was ended land-taking of all Iceland.	But then all the land taking of Iceland had ended.
Sá maður bjó þá að Hofi í Vopnafirði er hét Steinbjörn og var kallaður körtur og hafði honum þar land gefið Eyvindur föðurbróðir hans, allt á milli Vopnafjarðarár og Vesturdalsár.	The man lived then at Hof in Vopnafjord was named Steinbjorn and was called Kartur and had he there land given Eyvind father-brother his, all in between Vopnafjord and Vesturdalsa.	There was a man living at Hof in Vopnafjord named Steinbjorn. He was called Kartur and he had been given land there by his uncle eyvind, between Vopnafjord and Vesturadalsa.
Steinbjörn var eyðslumaður mikill í búinu.	Steinbjorn was spending-man much in estate.	Steinbjorn spent much on his estate.

En er Þorsteinn vissi það að lönd öll voru numin áður fór hann á fund Steinbjarnar og kaupir hann að honum land og reisir bæ á Tóftavelli og bjó þar nokkura vetur og varð honum gott til fjár og metnaðar.

But when Thorstein knew it that lands all were taken before travelled he to find Steinbjorn and bought he to him land and raised farm at Toftavellir and dwelt there some winters and became he good to wealth and ambition.

But when Thorstein knew that the lands were all taken before, he travelled to find Steinbjorn and bought land from him and raised a farm at Toftavellir, and stayed there several winters, and he became good in wealth and ambition.

Hann hafði skamma stund í búi verið áður hann fór og leitaði sér ráðs og bað konu þeirrar er Ingibjörg hét og var hún dóttir Hróðgeirs hins hvíta Hrafnssonar.

He had short while at estate been before he went and sought him advice and proposed-to woman there who Ingibjorg named and was she daughter Hrodgeir the white son-of-Hrafn.

He had been at the estate a short while when he sought the hand of a woman who was named Ingibjorg, and she was the daughter of Hrodgeir the White, son of Hrafn.

Hennar fékk hann.

Her married he.

He married her.

Við þessari konu átti hann fimm börn.

With this wife had he five children.

With this wife he had five children.

Sonur hans hét Önundur en annar Þórður, þriðji Þorgils.

Son his named Onund but another Thord, third Thorgils.

His son was named Onund, another Thord, and the third Thorgils.

Dætur hans hétu Þorbjörg og Þóra.

Daughters his named Thorbjorg and Thora.

His daughters were named Thorbjorg and Thora.

Þorgils var hinn mannvænlegasti maður.

Thorgils was the man-most-promising man.

Thorgils was the most promising man.

Þorsteinn græddi fé í ákafa.

Thorstein profited wealth with zeal.

Thorstein built up his wealth with zeal.

Steinbirni kört varð féfátt og fór á fund Þorsteins og beiddist fjárláns af honum.

Steinbjorn short was money-few and went he to-meet Thorstein's and to-ask fee-loan of him.

Steinbjorn was short of money and went to meet Thorstein to ask him for a loan.

Þorsteinn er og góður af fjárláninu og þangað til tekur hann lán af Þorsteini að harðla mjög eyðist fé Steinbjarnar og þykir Þorsteini versna skuldunauturinn og þykir óvís skuldastaðurinn að Steinbirni.

Thorstein was also good of fee-loaning and from-there to take him loan from Thorstein to harden much spending wealth Steinbjorn's and considered Thorstein worst debtor and seemed uncertain debt to Steinbjorn.

Thorstein was good to lend him money, and Steinbjorn spent this wealth so much that Thorstein considered him the worst debtor, and it seemed uncertain if Steinbjorn would repay his debt.

Og nú heimtir hann féið og lýkst með því þeirra fjárreiður að Steinbjörn geldur Þorsteini Hofland og fór Þorsteinn byggðum til Hofs og kaupir sér goðorð og gerist hinn mesti sveitarhöfðingi.

And now demanded he fee and ended with therefore their finances that Steinbjorn paid Thorstein Hofland and travelled Thorstein settlements to Hof and bought himself chieftan and was the best rural-chief.

And now he demanded the money to settle their finances, and so it was that Steinbjorn paid Thorstein with the land Hof, and Thorstein travelled to Hof and bought himself a chieftaincy, and he was the best rural chief.

Hann var allra manna vinsælastur.

He was all people popular.

He was popular with all the people.

Og er Þorsteinn hafði búið marga vetur að Hofi þá gerðust þau tíðindi að herbergjum hans að Ingibjörg tók sótt og andaðist.

And when Thorstein had lived many winters at Hof then made the tidings at rooms his that Ingibjorg took sickness and died.

And when Thorstein had lived for many winters at Hof, then the news at his household was that Ingibjorg took sickness and died.

Þorsteini þótti þetta skaði mikill en hélt þó búi sínu sem áður.

Thorstein thought this loss great but held though estate his as before.

Thorstein thought this loss great, but continued to hold his estate as before.

2

2

2

Maður hét Þórir.

Man named Thori.

There was a man named Thori.

Hann var sonur Atla er bjó í Atlavík fyrir austan vatn.

He was son-of Atli who lived in Atlavik before east water.

He was the son of Atli who lived in Atlavik before the east water.

Þar eru nú sauðhús.

There were now sheep-house.

There are now sheep houses there.

Þórir var kvongaður.

Thori was married.

Thori was married.

Kona hans hét Ásvör og var dóttir Brynjólfs hins gamla.

Wife his names Asvor and was daughter Brynolf's the old.

His wife's name was Asvor who was the daughter of Brynolf the Old.

Þau Þórir áttu tvö börn.

Then Thori had two children.

Then Thori had two children.

Hét sonur þeirra Einar en Ásvör dóttir.

Named son theirs Einar and Asvor daughter.

Their son was named Einar, and their daughter Asvor.

Einar var vasklegur og eigi stór maður, hávaðamaður mikill og í meðallagi vinsæll.

Einar was diligent and not great man, a-loud-man much and of middle-lying popularity.

Einar was diligent but not a large man, a loud man and of moderate popularity.

Ásvör var kvenna vænst og vinsælust.

Asvor was woman fair and popular.

Asvor was a fair woman and was popular.

Það gerðist til tíðinda á hag Þorsteins hvíta að hann tók augnaverk svo mikinn að þar fyrir missti hann sjónina,	It became to news that benefit Thorstein's white that he took eye-injury so much that there before lost his sight,	It became news that Thorstein the White had an injury in his eyes, so much that he lost his sight.
þykist vanfær til umsýslu, ræðir nú um við Þorgils, biður hann taka við liðinu.	seemed disabled to administration, discussed now about with Thorgils, bid he take with team.	He considered himself disabled in his administration, he now discussed with Thorgils, asking him to take over.
Þorgils sagði það skylt að hann veitti slíkt fulltingi er hann má.	Thorgils said it should that he grant such assistance as he may.	Thorgils said that it should be that he grant him any assistance that he may.
Faðir hans ræðir við hann að hann fái sér kvonfang og biðji Ásvarar Þórisdóttur.	Father his discussed with him that he get himself wife and asked Asvar Daughter-of-Thorri.	His father discussed with him that he should get himself a wife, and ask for the hand of Asvar, daughter of Thorri.
Og það varð og fór hún með honum til búsins og tókust með þeim ástir góðar og áttu tvö börn.	And it became and travelled she with him to farm and took with them love good and had two children.	And so it became, and she travelled with him to the farm and they took to loving each other well and had two children.
Sonur þeirra hét Helgi en dóttir Guðrún.	Son theirs named Helgi and daughter Gudrun.	Their son was named Helgi, and their daughter Gudrun.
Þorgils var þá vel tuttugu vetra.	Thorgils was then well twenty winters.	Thorgils was then twenty winters old.

3 3 3

Hrani hét maður og var kallaður gullhöttur.	Hrani named man and was called gold-hat.	There was a man named Hrani who was called Gold Hat.
Hann var fóstri Þorgils en frændi Ásvarar.	He was fosterer Thorgils but cousin Asvar's.	He was foster father to Thorgils and a cousin of Asvar's.
Hann var hávaðamaður mikill og var heimamaður að Hofi og var kallaður grályndur.	He was a-loud-man much and was home-man of Hof and was called gralyndr.	He was very much a loud man, and was of the household at Hof, and was called malicious.
Þorkell hét maður og var kallaður flettir.	Thorkell named man and was called flettir.	There was a man named Thorkell, and he was called Fleecer.
Hann var heimamaður að Hofi og frændi þeirra Hofverja, mikill og sterkur.	He was home-man of Hof and kinsman theirs of-Hof, great and strong.	He was a man of the household at Hof, and a kinsman of theirs, he was great and strong.

Old Icelandic	Literal	Translation
Þorbjörn hét maður.	Thorbjorn named man.	There was a man named Thorbjorn.
Hann bjó í Sveinungsvík.	He lived in Sveinungsvik.	He lived in Sveinungsvik.
Það er á milli Melrakkasléttu og Þistilsfjarðar.	It was in between Melrakkasletta and Thistilsfjord.	It was inbetween Melrakkasletta and Thistilsfjord.
Þorbjörn var drengur góður og rammur maður að afli, vinur góður Þorsteins hvíta.	Thorbjorn was fellow good and strong man of force, friend good Thorstein's white.	Thorbjorn was a good fellow, and a strong man of force, and a good friend of Thorstein the White.
Maður er nefndur Þorfinnur.	Man was named Thorfin.	There was a man named Thorfin.
Hann bjó að Skeggjastöðum í Hnefilsdal.	He lived at Skeggjastadir in Hnefilsdal.	He lived in Skeggjastadir in Hnefilsdal.
Hann átti og enn annað bú.	He had and one other estate.	He had also another estate.
Þorgerður hét kona hans.	Thorgerd named wife his.	His wife was named Thorgerd.
Þau áttu þrjá sonu og hét Þorsteinn sonur þeirra og var kallaður fagri, annar Einar, þriðji Þorkell.	Then had three sons and named Thorstein son theirs and was called fair, another Einar, third Thorkell.	Then they had three sons, their son was named Thorstein who was known as the Fair, another was Einar, and the third Thorkell.
Allir voru þeir mannvænlegir.	All were they men-promising.	They were all promising men.
Þorsteinn var fyrir þeim bræðrum.	Thorstein was before them brothers.	Thorstein was the leader of the brothers.
Hann var fullkominn að aldri er hér er komið sögunni.	He was full-coming of age as here was coming the-saga.	He was coming of age as here the story comes.
Kraki hét maður og bjó hann á þeim bæ er heitir á Krakalæk.	Kraki named man and lived he at that farm was named of Krakalaek.	There was a man named Kraki, and he lived at a farm named Krakalaek.
Kraki var vel auðigur maður, kvongaður maður og hét kona hans Guðrún.	Kraki was well wealthy man, married man and named wife his Gudrun.	Kraki was a wealthy man, a married man, and his wife's name was Gudrun.
Þau áttu dóttur eina barna er Helga hét og var allra kvenna fríðust og þótti sá kostur bestur í Fljótsdalshéraði.	Then had daughter one children was Helga named and was all women most-beautiful and seemed so choice best among Fljotsdalsheradi.	They had only one child, a daughter named Helga, and she was the most beautiful of all women, and so it seemed the best choice among the district of Fljotsdal.

Þess er getið að Þorsteinn fagri beiddist fjárlánstillaga af föður sínum og kvaðst vilja fara af landi á brott.	This was told-of that Thorstein fair asked loan-proposal from father his and said willed travel of land and away.	It was told that Thorstein the Fair asked for a loan from his father, saying that he wished to travel to lands far away.
Þorfinnur kvað svo vera skyldu.	Thorfin said so be should.	Thorfin said that so it should be.
Leggur hann til slíkt sem hann beiddist.	Laid he to such as he asked.	He gave him such as he asked for.
Hefir hann verið í förum nokkur sumur,	Had he been about travelling some summers,	He had been travelling about for several summers,
verður honum gott til fjár og metnaðar og hvert sinn er hann var utan lagði hann nokkuð eftir af fjárhlut þeim er hann þóttist þurfa og faðir hans.	became him good to wealth and ambition and each that when he was out-of left he some behind of fee-lot they as he thought needed and father his.	He became good in wealth and ambition, and each time that he went out, he kept behind some money that he thought he and his father would need.
Og eitt vor er Þorsteinn var út hér um veturinn kemur Einar Þórisson að máli við föður sinn og beiðist af honum tillags og segist vilja fara til félags við Þorstein.	And one spring when Thorstein was back here about winter came Einar son-of-Thorri to speak with father his and asked of him proposal and said willed travel to company with Thorstein.	And one spring when Thorstein was back here around winter, came Einar son of Thorri to speak with his father, he asked him about his proposal to travel in company with Thorstein.
Þorsteinn kvaðst eigi mundu synja Einari félags og gefur honum skip hálft og telur þó að honum segi í meðallagi hugur um félag þeirra fyrir sakar óvinveitts skaplyndis Einars.	Thorstein said not would refuse Einar company and gave him ship half-share and counted though that he said that middle-lying thought about company theirs for sake-of unfriendly temper Einar's.	Thorstein said that he would not refuse Einar the company, and he gave him a half share of the ship. He counted himself only moderately eager about their company for the sake of Einar's unfriendly temper.
Þeir fóru utan og lögðu félag saman.	They went out and laid company together.	They went out and had their company together.
Þorsteinn heldur öllu til virðingar Einari og virti hann í öllu mest og þó lagðist svo að Þorsteinn var meira virður en Einar af öðrum mönnum fyrir þess sakar að hann reyndist góður drengur og vinveittur í skaplyndi.	Thorstein held all to worthiness Einar and valued him to all most and though lay so that Thorstein was more respect than Einar of other people for this sake that he turned-out good fellow and friendly in temper.	Thorstein held Einar in worthiness, and honoured him most in all things, and so it lay that Thorstein was more respected than Einar by other people, for the sake of the fact that he was a good fellow with a friendly temper.
Fór vel um stund félag þeirra.	Travelled well about awhile company theirs.	They travelled well for awhile in their company.

4	4	4
Það er sagt einn vetur að þeir voru utan hér fóstbræður að Þorfinnur kemur að máli við Þorstein, hvern hann ætlaði sinn ráðahag að sumri.	It was said one winter that they were out here foster-brothers at Thorfin came to speak with Thorstein, what he intended that proposed that summer.	It was said that one winter, the foster brothers were out, and that Thorfin came to speak with Thorstein, about what he proposed to do that summer.
Þorsteinn kveðst utan ætla.	Thorstein said out-of intended.	Thorstein said that he intended to be going out.
Þorfinnur kvaðst heldur vilja að hann tæki við búi með honum.	Thorfin said rather willed that he take with estate with him.	Thorfin said that he rather wished to take over the estate with him.
Þorsteinn svarar og sagðist engan hug hafa á því en kvað hann slíkt hafa af hans góssi sem hann vildi.	Thorstein answered and said none thoughts had about for but said he such had of his belongings which he wished.	Thorstein answered and said that he had no thoughts about it, but that he had all the belongings that he wished.
Þorsteinn hafði mikið fé í förum.	Thorstein had much wealth to travel.	Thorstein had much wealth to travel.
Þorfinnur lést hugsað hafa ráð fyrir honum og lést vilja biðja honum til handa Helgu Krakadóttur.	Thorfin let know had advice for him and let willed ask him for hand Helga's daughter-of-Kraka.	Thorfin let him know that he had advice for him, and that he wished for him to have the hand of Helga daughter of Kraka.
Þorsteinn kvað sér það ofráð er hún stóð ein til alls arfs eftir Kraka.	Thorstein said he that too-high was she stood alone to all inheritance after Kraki.	Thorstein said that he found this too much, because she alone stood to inherit Kraki's estate.
Þorfinnur kvað vera jafnræði bæði fyrir ættar sakar og mannanar.	Thorfin said be equally both for noble sake and accomplishment.	Thorfin said that it would be an equal match for their nobility and their prospects.
Fara þeir nú og vekja þetta mál við Kraka.	Went they now and awoke this matter with Kraki.	They now went and raised the matter with Kraki.
Hann kallar sér þetta vel að skapi.	He calls himself this well of mood.	He said that it was well to his liking.
Var þetta mál upp borið fyrir Helgu og fundust eigi afsvör í hennar máli.	Was this matter up borne for Helga and found not of-answer in her matter.	The matter was borne up with Helga and it found no refusal from her.
Voru þeir vottar að heitorði Þorsteins.	Were they witnesses to title Thorstein's.	There were then witnesses to Thorstein's proposal.

Þorsteinn vildi fara utan fyrst en ráð skyldi takast þá er hann kæmi aftur.	Thorstein willed travel out first as advice should take then when he came back.	Thorstein wished to travel out first and advised that it would take place when he came back.
Fara þeir Þorsteinn og Einar og tekur Þorsteinn skyrbjúg í hafi að því er þeir kalla og varð hann eigi liðfær.	Travelled they Thorstein and Einar and took Thorstein scurvy in sea as that was they called and was he not team-working.	Thorstein and Einar then travelled out to sea, and Thorstein took to scurvy, and he was not able to do any work for the team.
Menn hlógu að honum og var Einar upphafsmaður að því.	Men laughed at him and was Einar instigator of that.	Men laughed at him, and Einar was the instigator of that.
Og er þeir komu til Noregs leigðu þeir þar skemmu eina en gáfu engan gaum að Þorsteini.	And when they came to Norway rented they there storehouse one but gave none heed to Thorstein.	And when they came to Norway they rented a storehouse but paid no heed to Thorstein.
Hann lá þar allan vetur.	He laid there all winter.	He laid there all winter.
Einar spottar hann mjög og lét kveða um hann.	Einar mocked him much and let sang about him.	Einar mocked him very much, and composed verses about him.
Og um vorið hitti Einar Þorstein og biður hann fjárskiptis, lést vilja hafa einn skip og kvað sér þykja Þorsteinn ólíklegur til utanferðar.	And about spring met Einar Thorstein and asked him fee-exchange, let willed had alone ship and said he thought Thorstein unlikely to out-travel.	And about spring Einar met Thorstein and asked him for a deal, that he wished to have the ship alone, because he thought Thorstein was unlikely to travel out.
Þorsteinn kvað eigi fjarri því farið hafa sem hann gat um skaplyndi Einars.	Thorstein said not away then travel had which he got about mind Einar's.	Thorstein said that this had not gone away from what he had expected with Einar.
Þeir skipta um vorið fjárhlut svo að Einar kaus en Þorsteinn skipti úr rúmi sínu.	They divided about spring fee-lots so as Einar chose but Thorstein changed out-of room his.	About spring they divided their goods as Einar had chosen, but Thorstein did not emerge from his room.
Einar hlaut skipið og hélt til Íslands um sumarið.	Einar got ship and held to Iceland about summer.	Einar got the ship and set sail for Iceland about summer.
Og er hann kom út var hann spurður tíðinda.	And when he came back-from was he asked news.	When he came back, he was asked for news.
En hann kvaðst eigi kunna tíðindi greinilega að segja, kvað Þorstein eigi dauðan hafa verið sérlega en þó hefði hann eigi ólíklegur verið að hann mundi eigi aftur koma.	But he said not knowing news clearly to say, said Thorstein not dead at-sea became especially but though would-have he not unlikely be that he would not return come.	But he said that he did not know of any news to say clearly, saying that Thorstein was not dead at sea exactly, but he would be unlikely to return.

Einar reið til föður síns og svívirti mjög Þorstein í allri frásögu.	Einar rode to father his and dishonoured much Thorstein to all from-saying.	Einar rode to his father and dishonoured Thorstein in all that he said.
Um haustið kom skip af hafi í Reyðarfjörð.	About autumn came ships from sea in Reydarfjord.	About autumn ships came from sea to Reydarfjord.
Einar reið til skips og keypti að Austmanni að hann segði andlát Þorsteins og svo gerði hann og allir skipmenn.	Einar rode to ships and bought the Eastern-man that he said death Thorstein's and so made he and all ship-men.	Einar rode to the ships and bribed a Norwegian man to say that Thorstein had died, and so he did, and all the ship's men.
Einar kom heim og sagði andlát Þorsteins og kvað hann hafa fengið herfilegan dauða þann vetur.	Einar came home and said death Thorstein's and said he at-sea caught harrowing-like death that winter.	Einar came home and said of Thorstein's death, and said that he had caught a harrowing death at sea that winter.
5	5	5
Einar bað föður sinn að hann skyldi biðja Helgu Krakadóttur.	Einar asked father his that he would ask Helga's Daughter-of-Kraka.	Einar asked his father to ask for the hand of Helga daughter of Kraka.
Þórir kvað svo vera skyldu.	Thori said so be would.	Thori said that he would.
Nú fara þeir heiman og koma til Kraka og vekja bónorð við hann fyrir hönd Einars.	Now travelled they home and came to Kraki and awoke proposal with him for hand Einar's.	Now they travelled home and came to Kraki and brought up the proposal with him for Einar's hand.
Kraki kvaðst áður vilja vita til víss andlát Þorsteins en lést þá mundu gefa Einari konuna ef það væri áður til víss vitað.	Kraki spoke before willed know to sure death Thorstein's but let then would give Einar wife if that would-be before to surely know.	Kraki said that before he wished to know for sure of Thorstein's death, but then would give Einar a wife if that was surely known before.
Þórir kvað það eigi sannlegt að Einar væri vonbiðill þeirrar konu er skjótt var heitin Þorsteini.	Thori said it not true-like that Einar was hopeful their wife that quickly was named Thorstein.	Thori said that it was unjust since Einar was so hopeful for a wife and Thorstein had been so quickly named.
Kraki lét eigi gangast svör þessa máls.	Kraki let not go answer this matter.	Kraki did not let the answer go on the matter.
Fara þeir feðgar heim við svo búið og litlu síðar ríður Einar norður til Hofs og segir Þorgilsi bónorðið og kveður sér hafa verið neitað.	Travel they father-and-son home therefore so dwelling and little afterwards rode Einar north to Hof and told Thorgils's marriage-proposal and said that had been denied.	Then father and son travelled home to their dwellings, and a little afterwards Einar rode north to Hof and told Thorgils about the marriage proposal and how it had been denied.

Hrani var hjá og svaraði svo:	Hrani was beside and answered so:	Hrani was beside him and answered thus:
"Illa koma þér Einar í hald góðir frændur ef þú skalt eigi fá konu þessa", kvað honum og lítið stoða að vera í vináttu við Þorgils ef hann skyldi einskis meta þessa sneypu er Einari var ger.	"Ill comes to-you Einar if hold good kinsmen if you shall not get woman this", said he and little stood to be in friendship with Thorgils if he would not appreciate this shame that Einar was made.	"It comes badly to you Einar that you hold good kinsmen if you shall not get this woman", he said, and there is little standing in your friendship with Thorgils if he would not appreciate the shame that Einar was made.
Þorgils svarar:	Thorgils answered:	Thorgils answered:
"Mér virðist Kraki viturlega með fara og mundi eg svo gera ef eg ætti hans hlut".	"To-me seems Kraki wise-like with go and would I so do if I had his share".	"It seems to me that Kraki is wise to go with this, and I would do so if I had his share".
Satt eitt sagði Einar frá orðum Kraka en þó eggjaði Hrani Þorgils að fara með honum.	Truth alone said Einar from words Kraki but though urged Hrani Thorgils to travel with him.	Einar spoke the truth alone about Kraki's words, but though Hrani urged Thorgils to travel with him.
Þorgils kvað eigi létt hugur um segja þó að þessu ráði yrði komið í hendur honum.	Thorgils said not let thought about to-say though that this advice would come to hands his.	Thorgils said that he was not inclined to give advice, though the matter was in his hands.
Síðan fóru þeir og hittu Kraka og hafði hann hin sömu svör fyrir sér sem fyrr.	Afterwards went they and met Kraki and had he the same answer for as was before.	Afterwards they went and met Kraki, and he had the same answer as before.
Þorgils mælti þá:	Thorgils said then:	Thorgils then said:
"Vera má að þú ráðir dóttur þinni en eigi muntu svo undan setja að þú fáir eigi sakagiftir um annað".	"Be may that you advise daughter yours but not shall so under sit that you few not sake-given about anything-else".	"It may be that you advise your daughter, but you won't do it in such a way that you won't be penalised for anything else".
Kraki mælti:	Kraki said:	Kraki said:
"Eigi mun eg til þess hætta".	"Not will I to this leave".	"I do not wish to leave it to this".
Hann fastnaði þá dóttur sína Einari og hafði sjálfur brúðkaup inni.	He betrothed then daughter his Einar and had himself wedding the.	He then betrothed his daughter to Einar, and hosted the wedding himself.
Kraki skyldi vera úr öllum vanda um kaupbrigði við Þorstein.	Kraki should be out-of all problems about bargains with Thorstein.	Kraki was released of all issues regarding the agreements with Thorstein.

6	6	6
Það er frá Þorsteini að segja að honum batnaði.	It is from Thorstein to say that he improved.	It is now to say from Thorstein that his health improved.
Bjó hann skip sitt til Íslands og kom út næsta sumar eftir brúðkaupið í Reyðarfjörð og hafði selt Austmönnum skipið.	Prepared he ship his to Iceland and came out next summer after wedding in Reydarfjord and had sold Eastern-men ship.	He prepared his ship to go to Iceland and came out the following summer after the wedding in Reydarfjord, and had sold his ship to Norwegians.
Hann ætlaði til ráðahagsins við Helgu og láta af förum.	He intended to consult with Helga's and leave of travel.	He intended to consult with Helga, and take his leave of any more travelling.
Og er hann kom til Íslands frétti hann alla þessa ráðabreytni.	And when he came to Iceland heard he all this decision-conduct.	And when he came to Iceland he heard all about the conduct.
Fór hann þá til fundar við föður sinn og létu þó haldast skipsöluna eigi að síður.	Travelled he then to meet with father his and yet though held ship's-sale none the less.	Then he travelled to meet with his father, and held to the sale of his ship none the less.
Þorsteinn lét lítt á sér finna um þetta mál.	Thorstein let little of this found about the matter.	Thorstein let little be known of how he found the matter.
Hann keypti sér skip um veturinn er uppi stóð í Bulungarhöfn og bjó það að öllu.	He bought himself ship about winter which up stood in Bolungarhof and prepared it for all.	He bought himself another ship about winter, which stood up in Bolungarhof, and prepared it for all.
Bræður hans ætluðu með honum utan og urðu eigi búnir svo skjótt sem hann því að þeir fóru að fjárheimtingum sínum um héraðið.	Brothers his intended with him out-of and became not prepared so quickly as he because that they went of finances theirs about district.	His brothers intended to travel out with him, but were not prepared so quickly, because they went about the district calling in their debts.
Austmenn vesuðust illa er þeirra þurfti að bíða, bræðra Þorsteins, ef byr kæmi á.	Eastern-men felt badly if they needed to wait, brothers Thorstein's, if fair-wind came to.	The Norwegians felt bad that they needed to wait for Thorstein's brothers, even though there was a favourable wind.
Þorsteinn mælti þá:	Thorstein said then:	Then Thorstein said:

"Eg mun ríða frá skipi voru og hitta þá og biðja þá að þeir flýti sér en þér skuluð bíða mín hið skemmsta sjö nætur".	"I will ride from ship ours and meet then and ask then that they hurry themselves but you should wait for-me the shortest seven nights".	"I will ride from our ship and meet them then, and ask that they hurry themselves, but you shoulld wait for me at least seven nights".
Þorsteinn reið utan eftir Öxarfirði úr Bulungarhöfn og upp á Möðrudalsheiði og ofan til Vopnafjarðar og svo austur yfir Smjörvatnsheiði og svo yfir Jökulsá að brú og svo yfir Fljótsdalsheiði og austur yfir Lagarfljót og upp með fljótinu uns hann kom í Atlavík snemma morguns.	Thorstein rode out behind Oxarfjord from Bolungarhof and up to Modrudalsheidi and down to Vopnafjord and so east over Smjorvatnsheidi and so over Jokulsla at bridge and so over Fljotsdalsheidi and east over Lagarfljot and up with river until he came to Atlavik early morning.	Thorsteinn rode out along Oxarfjord from Bolungarhof and up to Modrudalsheidi and down to Vopnafjord and so east over Smjorvatnsheidi and so over Fljotsdalsheidi and east over Lagarfljot and up along the river until he came to Atlavik early in the morning.
Þórir var farinn í skóg og húskarlar hans með honum ofan á Bulungarvöllu.	Thori was travelling to forest and house-carls his with him over to Bolungarvollu.	Thorir was traveling to the forest with his house-carls over to Bolungarvollu.
Einar var heima og var eigi upp risinn er Þorsteinn kom að durunum.	Einar was home and was not up risen when Thorstein came to door.	Einar was home and had not yet risen when Thorstein came to the door.
Kona var úti er Ósk hét.	Woman was about who Osk named.	There was a woman there named Osk.
Hún spurði hver hinn komni maður væri.	She asked who the coming man was.	She asked who the man who had come was.
Þorsteinn svarar:	Thorstein answered:	Thorstein answered:
"Sigurður heiti eg og á eg að gjalda Einari skuld og vil eg nú afhenda honum og gakk þú inn og vek Einar og bið hann út ganga".	"Sigurd named I and am I to debt Einar should and will I not of-hand him and go you then and wake Einar and ask him out going".	"I am named Sigurd and I should give my debt to Einar, and I wish to hand to him now, go you then and wake Einar up and ask him to come out".
Þorsteinn hafði spjót í hendi og ullhött á höfði.	Thorstein had spear in hand and woolen-hat on head.	Thorstein had a spear in his hand and a woolen hat on his head.
Konan vakti Einar.	Woman awoke Einar.	The woman awoke Einar.
Hann spurði hver kominn væri.	He asked who came was.	He asked who had come.
Hún sagði að hann nefndist Sigurður.	She said that he named Sigurd.	She said that he was named Sigurd.

Einar stóð þá upp og kippti skóm á fætur sér og tók skikkju yfir sig og gekk út síðan.	Einar stood then up and snatched shoes on feet his and took cloak over himself and went out afterwards.	Einar then stood up and snatched shoes on his feet, and took a cloak over himself and went out afterwards.
Og er hann kom út kenndi hann Einar að þar var kominn Þorsteinn og varð Einar nokkuð fár við.	And when he came out knew he Einar that there was come Thorstein and became Einar somewhat unresponsive with.	And when he came out Einar knew that Thorstein had come and Einar became unresponsive.
Þorsteinn mælti:	Thorstein spoke:	Thorstein spoke:
"Því em eg hér kominn að eg vil vita hverju er þú vilt bæta mér er þú gabbaðir skyrbjúg minn í hafi og hlóst að mér með hásetum þínum og mun eg vera allítilþægur að".	"Because am I here come that I will know how that you will compensate me as you mocked scurvy mine at sea and laughed at me with crew yours and shall I be all-little-quiet at".	"Because I have come here, I wish to know how you will compensate me for how you mocked me when I had scurvy at sea and laughed at me with your crew, and I shall be quiet".
Einar mælti:	Einar spoke:	Einar spoke:
"Heimtu fyrst að öllum þeim er hlógu að þér.	"Demand first that all they who laughed at you.	"Demand first from all those who laughed at you.
Eg mun þá bæta þér ef allir bæta aðrir".	I will then compensate you if all compensate others".	I will then compensate you if all others compensate".
Þorsteinn svarar:	Thorstein answered:	Thorstein answered:
"Eg em ekki svo féþurfa að eg nenni alla að sækja og vil eg að þú bætir fyrir þig".	"I am not so fee-needing that I care all to seek and will I that you compensate for you".	"I am not so much in need of money that I care at all to seek, and I wish that you compensate for you".
Einar kveðst eigi bæta mundu og sneri hann undan og til svefnskemmunnar.	Einar said not compensate would and turned he away and to sleeping-room.	Einar said that he would not compensate and he turned away to go to his room.
Þorsteinn bað hann bíða og hrapa eigi svo skjótt til rekkjunnar Helgu.	Thorstein bid him wait and hurried not so quickly to bed Helga's.	Thorstein bid him wait, and not hurry so quickly to Helga's bed.
Einar gaf engan gaum að því er hann mælti.	Einar gave none heed to then as he spoke.	Einar gave no need to him then as he spoke.
Síðan lagði Þorsteinn að Einari með spjótinu og í gegnum hann.	Afterwards laid Thorstein to Einar with spear and to through him.	Afterwards Thorstein laid towards Einar with a spear and it went through him.
Einar féll dauður inn í skemmuna.	Einar fell dead in about sleeping-room.	Einar fell dead into the room.

Þorsteinn bað griðkonuna greiða ferð Einars.	Thorstein asked house-maiden assistance travel Einar's.	Thorstein asked the house maiden to speed Einar on his way.
Þorsteinn ríður þá hina sömu leið aftur er hann reið fram.	Thorstein rode then the same way back as he rode from.	Thorstein then rode the same way back as he had rode from.
Hann reið vestur yfir háls til sels Þorbjarnar er stóð í milli Melrakkasléttu og Ormsár.	He rode west across hills to shed Thorbjorn's which stood in between Melrakkasletta and Ormsa.	He rode west across the hills to Thorbjorn's shed which stood in between Melrakkasletta and Ormsa.
Hann spurði Þorbjörn ef bræður hans hefðu þar komið en Þorbjörn kvað það eigi vera.	He asked Thorbjorn if brothers his had there come but Thorbjorn said that not been.	He asked thorbjorn if his brothers had come out there, but Thorbjorn said they had not been.
Þorsteinn sagði honum tíðindin og bað hann segja bræðrum sínum að þeir flýttu sér til skips.	Thorstein told him news and bid he tell brothers his that they hurry themselves to ship.	Thorstein told him the news and bid that he tell his brothers, that they hurry themselves to the ship.
Reið Þorsteinn þá til skips.	Rode Thorstein then to ship.	Then Thorstein rode to the ship.
Griðkona gerði honum Þóri orð og lét segja honum víg Einars sonar síns og brá Þórir skjótt við og fór norður til Vopnafjarðar með tvo húskarla sína og fór á skipi yfir fljót og til Hofs.	The-house-keeper gave him Thori word and let tell him killing Einar's son his and startled Thori quickly with and travelled north to Vopnafjord with two house-carls his and travelled by ship across river and to Hof.	The housekeeper sent word to Thori and told him about the killing of his son Einar, and Thori was quick and traveled north to Vopnafjord with two of his house-carls and travelled by ship across the river and to Hof.
Sagði hann þeim Hofsmönnum víg Einars.	Told he the Men-of-Hof killing Einar's.	He told the men of Hof about Einar's killing.
Þorgils kvað sér eigi vel hafa hug um sagt þegar er Einar fékk Helgu.	Thorgils said he not well have thought about said when that Einar married Helga.	Thorgils said that he did not think well of when it was said thast Einar married Helga.
Þeir báðu hann eftir ríða.	They bid him after ride.	They bid him to ride after them.
Hann lét þá taka hesta sína.	He had then take horses theirs.	He then had his horses fetched.
Hrani frýði honum áður hugar ef hann seinkaði ferðinni.	Hrani persuaded him about mind if he delayed travelling.	Hrani persuaded him about his thoughts if he delayed travelling.

Þórir hvarf aftur og gerði það að ráði Þorgils en húskarlar hans fóru með Þorgilsi og voru þeir sjö saman og fóru síðan leið sína.	Thori disappeared again and did that at advice Thorgils but house-carls his went with Thorgils's and were they seven together and travelled afterwards way theirs.	Thori disappeared again and did as Thorgils had advised him, but his house-carls went with Thorgils and they were seven together, and afterwards they travelled on their way.
7	7	7
Bræður Þorsteins ríða til sels Þorbjarnar annan morgun eftir er Þorsteinn hafði þaðan riðið.	Brothers Thorstein's rode to shed Thorbjorn's next morning after that Thorstein had from-there rode.	Thorstein's brothers rode to Thorbjorn's shed the next day after Thorstein had ridden away.
Þeir höfðu þar dagverð en lögðust síðan niður til svefns.	They had there time-of-day-meal but laid afterwards down to sleep.	They had their breakfast but then afterwards laid down to sleep.
Þorbjörn latti þá þessa mjög því að hann sagði þeim víg Einars og orðsending Þorsteins en Þorbjörn var vinur hvorratveggja.	Thorbjorn discouraged then this much because that he told them killing Einar's and message Thorstein's but Thorbjorn was friend either-side.	Thorbjorn discouraged this greatly because he told them of Einar's killing, and Thorstein's message, and was a friend on either side.
Litlu síðar kom Þorgils og þeir sjö saman.	Little afterwards came Thorgils and they seven together.	A little afterwards Thorgils came with his men, and they were seven together.
Þorbjörn sagði þeim bræðrum að þeir Þorgils voru þar komnir og vakti hann þá.	Thorbjorn told they brothers at they Thorgils were there coming and awoke he then.	Thorbjorn told them brothers that Thorgils and his men were coming and he awoke them.
Hvergi máttu þeir undan komast.	Nowhere could they away-from come.	There was nowhere they could go to get away.
Þorbjörn réð þeim að þeir græfu þar djúpa gröf í selinu fyrir durunum "en eg mun standa í durunum".	Thorbjorn advised them that they dig there deep ditch about shed before door "but I will stand about door".	Thorbjorg advised them that they dig a deep trench around the shed before the door, "but I will stand in front of the door".
Og svo gerðu þeir.	And so did they.	And so they did.
Þeir Þorgils koma þá að selinu.	They Thorgils came then to shed.	Thorgils and his men then came to the shed.
Þóttist hann vita að þeir bræður mundu þar inni er hrossin voru mædd og nýkomin undan klyfjum.	Thought he knew that they brothers would there in be horses were tired and newly-arrived under hooves.	They thought they knew that the brothers were inside, because the horses were tired and newly unsaddled.

"Veit eg", segir Þorgils, "að þeir eru hér".	"Know i", said Thorgils, "at they are here".	"I know", said Thorgils, "that they are here".
Þorbjörn svarar:	Thorbjorn answered:	Thorbjorn answered:
"Þú ert maður glöggvastur en þó eru þeir bræður eigi hér sem þú segir.	"You are man sharpest but though are they brothers not here as you say.	"You are the sharpest of men, but though the brothers are not here as you say.
En eg lét fara eftir viðum hross mín og höfum nýtekið af þeim klyfjar.	But I let travel after wood horses mine and have newly-taken of them hoof.	But I travelled to get wood with my horses, and I have just taken off their hooves.
Eru þau nýkomin frá veturhúsum en áður gengu þau af rekaströndum til skálagerðar í Sveinungsvík og á eg hrossin".	Are they newly-come from winter-house but before went they of rekastrondum to hut-make about Sveinungsvik and are mine horses".	They are newly come from the winter house, and before that they were on Rekastrondum to make a hut, and they are my horses".
Þorgils kvaðst eigi þessu trúa mundu "og far þú úr durunum og viljum vér rannsaka selið".	Thorgils said not this trusted should "and go you out-from door and will we search shed".	Thorgils said that he did not trust this "and you get away from the door, and we will search the shed".
Þorbjörn kvaðst eigi það gera mundu "síðan þér trúið eigi minni tilsögu".	Thorbjorn said not that done would-be "since you trust not less to-say".	Thorbjorm said that it would not be done "since you will not trust what I say".
Hrani mælti:	Hrani spoke:	Hrani spoke:
"Drepum hann þá ef hann vill eigi fara úr durunum".	"Kill-we him then if he will not go out-from door".	"Let us kill him if he will not go away from the door".
Þorgils svarar:	Thorgils answered:	Thorgils answered:
"Þá þykir föður mínum illa".	"Then think father mine badly".	"Then my father would think badly about that".
Þá bauð Þorkell flettir að fara á bak húsinu og hlaupa af vegginum ofan milli Þorbjarnar og duranna og bera hann svo frá durunum og ofan fyrir brekkuna.	Then offered Thorkell Fleecer to go to back of-the-house and jump of roof above between Thorbjorn and the-door and bear him so from the-door and over for slope.	Then Thorkell Fleecer offered to go to to the back of the house and jump off the roof above, between Thorbjorn and the-door, and bear him from the door and over the slope.
Þorgils bað hann svo gera.	Thorgils bid him so do.	Thorgils bid him to do so.
Síðan breytti Þorkell svo að Þorbjörn var með þessari aðferð borinn frá seldurunum.	After changed Thorkell so that Thorbjorn was with this method carried away from-the-hut-door.	Afterwards Thorkell changed so that Thorbjorn was carried away from the hut door.

Síðan bundu þeir hann.	After bound they him.	Afterwards they bound him.
Eftir það gengu þeir að durunum og mátust þeir um hver þeirra fyrst skyldi inn ganga.	After that went they to door and discussed they about who of-them first should in go.	After that they went to the doors and argued which of them should go in first.
En er Þorgils fann þetta mælti hann:	But when Thorgils found this spoke he:	But when Þorgils found this he spoke:
"Eigi verður oss nú hugmannlega er vér þorum eigi inn að ganga".	"Not become we now intelligent as we dare not to go in".	"We will not be wise now if we do not dare to enter".
Þorgils hleypur þá inn.	Thorgils ran then in.	Thorgils then ran in.
Þorbjörn aftaldi hann og sagðist letja hann inn að ganga en hann gaf engan gaum að orðum hans.	Thorbjorn of-told him and said discourage he in to go but he gave none heed that words his.	Þorbjörn dissuaded him and said he would discourage him to enter, but he paid no attention to his words.
Hann hafði skjöldinn yfir höfði sér.	He had shield over head his.	He had a shield over his head.
Hann snarar þá inn og hljóp í gröfina og drápu þeir bræður hann þar í gröfinni.	He sneaked then in and ran to ditch and killed they brothers him there in the-grave.	He then snuck in and ran into the ditch, and the brothers killed him there in the tomb.
Síðan rufu förunautar Þorgils selið og sóttu þá bræður um stundar sakar.	Afterwards tore companions Thorgils shed and sought then brothers about awhile sake.	Afterwards Thorgil's companions tore their way into the shed and pursued the brothers for a while.
Hrani gullhöttur lá á selvegginum og koglaði þann veg inn.	Hrani gold-hat lay about shed-ways and quivered he way in.	Hrani Gold Hat kay along the shed walls and found a way in.
Þá var hann lagður spjóti í höndina.	Then was he laid spear in hand.	Then he had a spear in his hand.
Þeir bræður vörðust bæði vel og drengilega en féllu báðir þar að síðustu með góðan orðstír.	They brothers guarded both well and fellow-like but fell both there at finally with good reputation.	The brothers both defended themselves wel, but then fell there finally with good reputation.
Þar féllu og báðir húskarlar Þóris og hinn þriðji maður, Þorgils Þorsteinsson, er þá var þrítugur að aldri.	There fell and both house-carls Thorir and the third man, Thorgils son-of-Thorstein, as then was thirty of age.	There two house-carls of Thorir also fell, and Thorgils son of Thorstein, who was then thirty in age.

Þorbjörn var leystur síðan eftir fundinn.	Thorbjorn was loosened since after found.	Thorbjorn was released afterwards.
Hann færði alla vöru þeirra bræðra í Bulungarhöfn til skips og sagði Þorsteini tíðindin.	He took all wares theirs brothers in Bolungarhof to ship and said Thorstein news.	He took all of the brothers' belongings to the ship in Bolungarhof and told Thorstein the news.
Þorsteinn kvað Þorbjörn þetta vel gert hafa og skiljast með mikilli vináttu.	Thorstein said Thorbjorn that well done had and separated with much friendship.	Thorstein said that Thorbjorn had done well and they separated with good friendship.
Þorsteinn fór utan um sumarið og var á brottu fimm vetur.	Thorstein went out-of about summer and was to away five winters.	Thorstein went abroad that summer and was away for five winters.
Kom hann sér vel við höfðingja og þótti hinn röskvasti maður.	Came he himself well with chieftans and thought the most-mature man.	He had the favour of the chieftains and was thought of as the most mature man.
Hrani gullhöttur kom heim til Hofs og sagði Þorsteini hvíta að synir Þorfinns tveir væru fallnir og húskarlar Þóris tveir.	Hrani gold-hat came home to Hof and told Thorstein white that sons Thorfin's two were fallen and house-carls Thorir two.	Hrani Gold-Hat came home to Hof and told Thorstein the White that Thorfin's two sons were fallen and Thorir's two house-carls.
Þorsteinn spurði:	Thorstein asked:	Thorstein asked:
"Hvar er Þorgils sonur minn?"	"Where is Thorgils son mine?"	"Where is my son Thorgils?"
Hrani svarar:	Hrani answered:	Hrani answered:
"Hann er og fallinn líka".	"He was and fallen alike".	"He was also fallen".
Þorsteinn mælti:	Thorstein said:	Thorstein said:
"Fjandlega segir þú frá tíðindum.	"Fiendishly say you from news.	"You bring fiendish news.
Illt hefir jafnan af þér hlotist og þínum ráðum".	Ill has equally of your lot and your advice".	Ill has always been your lot and your advice".
Þetta þótti mönnum mikil tíðindi þá er spurðust.	That seemed men much news then was learned-of.	It seemed much when people learned the news of it.

Um sumarið eftir voru mál til búin á hendur Þorsteini Þorfinnssyni og varð hann sekur um víg Einars.	About summer after were matters to prepared at hand Thorstein son-of-Thorfin and became he guilty about killing Einar's.	About the following summer, a case was prepared against Thorstein son of Thorfin, and he was found guilty of Einar's killing.
Brodd-Helgi var þá þrevetur er faðir hans var drepinn og var þá þegar efnilegur maður að jöfnum aldri.	Brodd-Helgi was then three-winters when father his was killed and was then already promising man of equal age.	Spike-Helgi was then three winters old when his father was kiled, and was then already a promising for his age.
Þorsteinn Þorfinnsson fór til Íslands að fimm vetrum liðnum og kom skipi sínu í Miðfjörð.	Thorstein son-of-Thorfin travelled to Iceland at five winters passed and came ship his to Midfjord.	Thorstein son-of-Thorgin travelled to Iceland five winters later, and his ship came to Mifdjord.
Hann reið þegar norður til Hofs við fimmta mann.	He rode then north to Hof with five men.	He rode then north to Hof with five men.
Brodd-Helgi var þá átta vetra gamall og lék sér á hlaðinu úti og bauð þeim öllum þar að vera.	Brodd-Helgi was then eight winters old and played he about farmyard outside and invited them all there to be.	Spike-Helgi was then eight winters old and he played about the farmyard outside and invited them all in.
Þorsteinn spurði hví hann laðaði gesti.	Thorstein asked why he attracted guests.	Thorstein asked how it was that he invited guests.
Hann kvaðst þar allt eiga með afa sínum.	He spoke there all owned with grandfather his.	He spoke that all there was owned by his grandfather.
Þeir Þorsteinn Þorfinnsson gengu inn eftir það.	They Thorstein son-of-Thorfin went in after that.	Thorstein son-of-Thorfin and his men went in after that.
Þorsteinn hvíti kenndi farmanna daun og spurði hverjir komnir væru.	Thorstein white knew farmers death and asked why came were.	Thorstein the White knew of the farmers death and asked why they had come.
Þorsteinn Þorfinnsson segir hið sanna.	Thorstein son-of-Thorfin said the truth.	Thorstein son-of-Thorgin told him the truth.
Þorsteinn hvíti mælti:	Thorstein white spoke:	Thorstein the White spoke:
"Hvort þótti þér of lítil mín skapraun ef þú sóttir mig eigi heim, blindan karl og gamlan?"	"Either thought you of little my temperament if you sought me not home, blind man and old".	"Either you thought little of my trials, if you sought me at home, a blind old man".
Þorsteinn Þorfinnsson svarar:	Thorstein son-of-Thorfin answered:	Thorstein son-of-Thorfin answered:

"Eigi gekk mér það til heldur hitt að eg vil bjóða þér sjálfdæmi fyrir Þorgils son þinn og hefi eg ærið góss til þess að bæta hann svo að eigi hafi annar maður dýrri verið".	"Not going to-me that to rather other that I will bid you self-example for Thorgils son yours and have I considerable estate to this that compensate he so that not had another man precious made".	This was not my thought, rather the opposite, that I wish to bid you self-judgement for Thorgils, your son, and I have considerable estate for this to compensate for him, so much that no other man has been paid".
Þorsteinn hvíti kvaðst eigi vilja bera Þorgils son sinn í sjóði.	Thorstein white spoke not will bear Thorgils son his to funds.	Thorstein the White said that he did not wish to bear his son Thorgil in his purse.
Þorsteinn Þorfinnsson og var kallaður Þorsteinn fagri,	Thorstein son-of-Thorfin and was called Thorstein fair,	Thorstein son of Thorfin was called Thorstein the Fair.
hann sprettur þá upp og leggur höfuð sitt í kné Þorsteini hvíta nafna sínum.	he sprang then up and laid head his about knee Thorstein white namesake his.	He jumped then up and laid his head on the knee of Thorstein the White, his namesake.
Þorsteinn hvíti svarar þá:	Thorstein white answered then:	Thorstein the White then answered:
"Eigi vil eg láta höfuð þitt af hálsi slá.	"Not will I let head yours off neck struck.	"I will not let your head be struck from your neck".
Munu þar eyru sæmst sem uxu.	Shall then ears same as grow.	Your ears will become you better where they grow.
En þá geri eg sætt okkar í millum að þú skalt fara hingað til Hofs til umsýslu með allt þitt og ver hér meðan eg vil en þú sel skip þitt".	But then make I settlement ours in between that you shall travel here to Hof to administrations with all yours and be here with I will but you sell ship yours".	But then I make this our settlement, that you shall travel here to Hof with all your people, and be here as long as I am, having sold your ship.
Þessari sætt játar Þorsteinn fagri.	This settlement accepts Thorstein fair.	Thorstein the Fair accepted this settlement.
Og er þeir kumpánar gengu út lék sveinninn Helgi Þorgilsson sér að gullreknu spjóti er Þorsteinn fagri hafði sett hjá durunum er hann gekk inn.	And as they companions went out played boy Helgi son-of-Thorgils with a gold-plated spear as Thorstein fair had set beside door as he went in.	And as Thorstein and his companions went outside, the boy Helgi son of Thorgil played with a gold plated spear that was set beside the door when he went in.
Þorsteinn fagri mælti við Helga:	Thorstein fair spoke with Helga:	Thorstein the Fair spoke with Helga.
"Viltu þiggja að mér spjótið?"	"Will-you accept of my spear?"	"Will you accept my spear?"

Helgi ræðst þá um við Þorstein hvíta fóstra sinn hvort hann skyldi þiggja spjótið að Þorsteini fagra.	Helgi decided then about with Thorstein white foster his whether he should receive spear at Thorstein fair.	Helgi then decided about this with Thorstein the White's foster father whether he should accept the spear of Thorstein the Fair.
Þorsteinn hvíti svarar, bað hann þiggja víst og launa sem best.	Thorstein white answered, bid he receive certainly and repay as best.	Thorstein the White answered, inviting him to certainly receive and repay the gift as best he could.
Þorsteinn fagri var eina nótt að Hofi í það sinni.	Thorstein fair was one night at Hof about that his.	Thorstein the Fair was in Hof for one night on that occasion.
Þorsteinn fagri fór til skips síns og seldi það.	Thorstein fair travelled to ship his and sold it.	Thorstein the Fair travelled to his ship and sold it.
Síðan færði hann sig til Hofs í Vopnafjörð með allt sitt.	Afterwards took he himself to Hof in Vopnafjord with all his.	Afterwards he took himself to Hof in Vopnafjord with all his companions.
Hann færði mjög fram kvikfé Þorsteins hvíta nafna síns.	He took much from wealth Thorstein's white namesake his.	He greatly advanced the wealth of his namesake, Thorstein the White.
En er hann hafði þar verið nokkura stund þá vildi Þorsteinn hvíti að Þorsteinn nafni hans bæði Helgu Krakadóttur og svo gerði hann.	And as he had there been some while then willed Thorstein white at Thorstein namesake his both Helga's Daughter-of-Kraka and so did he.	And when he had been there for some time, Thorstein the White willed his namesake to ask for the hand of Helga daughter of Kraka, and so he did.
Þorsteinn hvíti var í ferð með honum og gengu þau mál vel fram og þótti Kraka þetta gert eftir sínu skaplyndi.	Thorstein white was about journey with him and went then matter well from and thought Kraki that made after his temperament.	Thorstein the White journeyed with him, and the matter went well, with Kraki finding it well with his liking.
Fór Helga þá til Hofs með Þorsteini fagra því að Þorsteinn hvíti vildi brúðkaupið inni hafa því að hann þóttist hrumur til að fara að sækja brúðkaupið annars staðar og af því var svo gert.	Travelled Helga then to Hof with Thorstein fair since that Thorstein white willed wedding the at-sea since that he thought decrepit to that travel at seek wedding another place and of then was so done.	Helga then went to Hof with Thorstein the Fair because Thorstein the White wanted the wedding inside, because he thought it was too late to attend the wedding elsewhere, and so it was done.
Boðið fór vel fram.	Invitation went well from.	The invitation went well.
Voru samfarar þeirra góðar.	Was interaction theirs good.	Their interaction was good.

Átta vetur var Þorsteinn fagri að Hofi með nafna sínum og var honum í sonar stað í allri umsýslu.	Eight winters was Thorstein fair at Hof with namesake his and was him his son's place about all administered.	For eight winters Thorstein the Fair was at Hof with his namesake, and was a son to him in all his dealings.
Og þá er svo var komið tímum mælti Þorsteinn hvíti til nafna síns:	And then was so was come time spoke Thorstein white to namesake his:	And when the time had come, Thorstein the White said to his namesake:
"Vel hefir þú gefist mér og ertu röskur maður og drengur góður um alla hluti og vel að þér búinn.	"Well have you given me and are-you strong man and fellow good about all things and well that you prepared.	"Well you have given yourself to me and you are a strong man and a good man in all things and well done.
Nú vil eg að þú bregðir þessu ráði og svo föður þíns og Kraka mágs þíns og ráðist allir til utanferðar með allt það er þér eigið því að eg ætla Helga frænda mínum og fóstra gerast mjög þungt til þín.	Now wish I that you action this advice and so father yours and Kraki brother-in-law yours and advise all to out-travel with all it as you own because that I suppose Helga kinsman mine and fosterer will-be very unhappy to you.	Now I wish that you action this advice, your father, and Kraki your father-in-law. I advise you to all travel out with all that you own, because Helgi my kinsman and foster son will be very unhappy towards you.
En hann er nú átján vetra gamall.	But he is now eighteen winters old.	But he is now eighteen winters old.
En það er líkast að eg verði maður ekki langlífur héðan af en eg vildi að við skildumst vel en Helgi frændi minn mun verða ofsamaður mikill og engi jafnaðarmaður.	But it was like that I be man not long-life from-here of but I will that with parted well but Helgi kinsman mine will be over-bearing-man much and none equally-man.	But it seems that I will not be a long-lived man from now on, but I would like us to get along well, but my kinisman Helgi will be a great overbearing man and not an equal man.
Nú haf þú ráð mitt um þetta og ver hér eigi lengur en eg legg ráð til".	Now have you advice mine about this and be here no longer than I lay advice to".	Now that you have my advice about this, be here no longer than I advise you to".
Þorsteinn fagri kvað svo vera skyldu.	Thorstein fair said so be should.	Thorstein the Fair said that so it should be.
Þorsteinn fagri keypti tvö skip og fór utan með allt sitt skuldalið.	Thorstein fair bought two ships and travelled out-of with all his indebted.	Thorstein the Fair bought two ships and travelled abroad with all of his kinsmen.
Þorfinnur faðir hans fór og utan og Kraki mágur hans.	Thorfin father his travelled and out-of and Kraki brother-in-law his.	Thorfin his father travelled out, and his brother in law Kraki.

Þeir komu norðarlega við Noreg og fóru um sumarið eftir norður á Hálogaland og ílentust þar með öllu liði sínu.	They came northerly with Norway and travelled about summer after north to Halogaland and landed then with all company theirs.	They came to the north of Norway and travelled about the summer after to Halogaland and landed then with all their company.
Bjó Þorsteinn fagri þar á meðan hann lifði og þótti hinn vaskasti maður.	Lived Thorstein fair there as long-as he lived and thought-of the boldest man.	Thorstein the Fair lived there as long as he lived, and was thought of as the boldest man.
8	8	8
Helgi óx upp með Þorsteini hvíta fóstra sínum.	Helgi grew up with Thorstein white foster his.	Helgi grew up with Thorstein the White, his foster father.
Hann gerðist mikill maður og sterkur, bráðger, vænn og stórmannlegur og ekki málugur í barnæsku, ódæll og óvæginn þegar á unga aldri.	He became great man and strong, quick, kind and great-man-like and not talkative in childhood, unruly and ruthless already at young age.	He became a great and strong man, quick, kind, and generous, and not talkative in childhood, unruly and ruthless at a young age.
Hann var hugkvæmur og margbreytinn.	He was resourceful and many-varied.	He was resourceful in many varied ways.
Það var einn dag að Hofi er naut voru að stöðli,	It was one day at Hof when bulls were at standing,	It was one day at Hof when bulls were at the cowshed,
þar var griðungur einn kominn til nautanna, mikill og stór.	there was bull one coming to bull, great and large.	there one bull came, great and large.
Annar griðungur var heima fyrir, mikill og ógurlegur, er þeir frændur áttu.	Another bull was home before, great and formidable, as they kinsmen had.	Another bull was at the homestead, great and formidable, belonging to the kinsmen.
Helgi var þá úti staddur og sá að griðungarnir gengust að og stönguðust og varð heimagriðungurinn vanhluta fyrir búigriðunginum.	Helgi was then about standing and saw that bulls went to and stabbing and was home-bulls part for farm-bulls.	Helgi was standing outside and saw that the bulls went to and stabbed each other, the homestead bull and the farm bull.
En er Helgi sér það gengur hann inn og sækir sér mannbrodda stóra og bindur þá framan í ennið á heimagriðunginum.	But as Helgi saw it went he in and fetched himself man-shaft great and tied then in-front-of the head of home-bull.	But as Helgi saw it, he went in and fetched himself a great spike and tied it to the forehead of the homestead bull.
Síðan taka þeir til og stangast sem áður allt þar til er heimagriðungurinn stangar hinn til dauðs.	Afterwards took they to and stabbed as before all there until was home-bull stabbed him to death.	After this they took to stabbing each other as before, all until the homestead bull stabbed the other bull to death.

Höfðu mannbroddarnir gengið á hol.	Had spear gone into hole.	The spear had gone into a hole.
Þótti flestum mönnum þetta vera bellibragð er Helgi hafði gert.	Thought most people that had-been trick was Helgi had done.	Most people thought that this was a trick that Helgi had played.
Fékk hann af þessu það viðurnefni að hann var kallaður Brodd-Helgi en þá þótti mönnum það miklu heillavænlegra að hafa tvö nöfn.	Got he of this the nickname that he was called Brodd-Helgi but then thought people that much beneficial to have two names.	From this he got the nickname and was called Spike-Helgi, but then people thought it beneficial to have two names.
Var það þá átrúnaður manna að þeir menn mundu lengur lifa sem tvö nöfn hefðu.	Was it then believed men that they men would longer live which two names had.	It was then believed that men would live longer if they had two names.
Skjótt var það auðséð á Helga að hann mundi verða höfðingi mikill og engi jafnaðarmaður.	Soon was it easily-seen of Helga that he would become chief great and no-one equal-man.	It was soon easily seen of Helgi that he would become a great chieftain and an unequal man.
Einn vetur lifði Þorsteinn hvíti síðan er þeir Þorsteinn fagri skildu og þótti hann verið hafa hið mesta mikilmenni.	One winter lived Thorstein white afterwards as they Thorstein fair separated and thought he been had the most great-man.	Thorstein the White lived for one winter after Thorstein the Fair separated and he was thought to have been the greatest man.
Geitir í Krossavík átti Hallkötlu dóttur Þiðranda hins gamla Ketilssonar þryms, sonar Geitis og Hallkötlu.	Geitir in Krossavik married Hallkotla daughter Thidrandi the old son-of-Ketil thrymr, son Geitis and Hallkotla.	Geitir of Krossavik married Hallkotla daughter of Thidrandi the old, son of Ketil Thunder, son of Geitir and Hallkotla.
Með þeim Geiti og Brodd-Helga var vinátta mikil í fyrstu en minnkaðist svo sem á leið og varð úr fullur fjandskapur sem segir í Vopnfirðinga sögu.	With them Geiti and Brodd-Helgi was friendship much at first but lessened so as it passed and became from full fiendship as said in Vopnafjord saga.	When them Geiti and Spike-Helgi was friendship much at first, but lessened as it passed, and became enmity as told in Vopnafjord saga.
Og lýkur hér sögu Þorsteins hins hvíta.	and ends here saga Thorstein the white.	And here ends the saga of Thorstein the White.

Word List *(Old Icelandic to English)*

A, a

Old Icelandic	English
að	a, as, at, for, of, that, the, to
aðferð	method
aðrir	others
af	from, of, off
afa	grandfather
afhenda	of-hand
afli	force
afsvör	of-answer
aftaldi	of-told
aftur	again, back, return
aldri	age
alla	all
allan	all
allir	all
alllítilþægur	all-little-quiet
allra	all
allri	all
alls	all
allt	all
andaðist	died
andlát	death
annað	anything-else, other
annan	next
annar	another
annars	another
arfs	inheritance
Atla	Atli (name)
Atlavík	Atlavik (place)
auðigur	wealthy
auðséð	easily-seen
augnaverk	eye-injury
austan	east
austmanni	eastern-man
austmenn	eastern-men
austmönnum	eastern-men
austur	east

Á, á

Old Icelandic	English
á	about, am, and, are, as, at, by, he, in, into, it, of, on, that, to
áður	about, before
ákafa	zeal
ástir	love
Ásvarar	Asvar (name), asvar's
Ásvör	Asvor (name)
átján	eighteen
átrúnaður	believed
átta	eight
átti	had, married
áttu	had

Æ, æ

Old Icelandic	English
ærið	considerable
ætla	intended, suppose
ætlaði	intended
ætluðu	intended
ættar	noble
ætti	had

B, b

Old Icelandic	English
bað	asked, bid, proposed-to
báðir	both
báðu	bid
bæ	farm
bæði	both
bæta	compensate
bætir	compensate
bak	back
barna	born, children
barnæsku	childhood
batnaði	improved
bauð	invited, offered
beiddist	asked, to-ask
beiðist	asked
bellibragð	trick

Old Icelandic	English
bera	bear
best	best
bestur	best
bið	ask
bíða	wait
biðja	ask, ask
biðji	asked
biður	asked, bid
bindur	tied
bjó	dwelt, lived, prepared
bjóða	bid
blindan	blind
boðið	invitation
bónorð	proposal
bónorðið	marriage-proposal
borið	borne
borinn	carried
börn	children
brá	startled
bráðger	quick
bræðra	brothers
bræðrum	brothers
bræður	brothers
bregðir	action
brekkuna	slope
breytti	changed
Brodd-Helga	Brodd-Helgi (name)
Brodd-Helgi	Brodd-Helgi (name)
brott	away
brottu	away
brú	bridge
brúðkaup	wedding
brúðkaupið	wedding
Brynjólfs	Brynolf's (name)
bú	estate
búi	estate
búið	dwelling, lived
búigriðunginum	farm-bulls
búin	prepared
búinn	prepared
búinu	estate
Bulungarhöfn	Bolungarhof (place)
Bulungarvöllu	Bolungarvollu (place)
bundu	bound
búnir	prepared

Old Icelandic	English
búsins	farm
byggðum	settlements
byr	fair-wind

D, d

Old Icelandic	English
dætur	daughters
dag	day
dagverð	time-of-day-meal
dauða	death
dauðan	dead
dauðs	death
dauður	dead
daun	death
djúpa	deep
dó	died
dóttir	daughter
dóttur	daughter
drápu	killed
drengilega	fellow-like
drengur	fellow
drepinn	killed
drepum	kill-we
duranna	the-door
durunum	door, the-door
dýrri	precious

E, e

Old Icelandic	English
ef	if
efnilegur	promising
eftir	after, behind
eg	i, mine
eggjaði	urged
eiga	owned
eigi	no, none, not
eigið	own
ein	alone
eina	one
Einar	Einar (name)
Einari	Einar (name)
Einars	Einar's (name)
einn	alone, one
einskis	not

Old Icelandic	English
eitt	alone, one
ekki	not
em	am
en	and, but, than
engan	none
engi	none, no-one
enn	one
ennið	head
er	as, be, if, is, that, was, when, which, who
ert	are
ertu	are-you
eru	are, were
eyðist	spending
eyðslumaður	spending-man
eyru	ears
Eyvindur	Eyvind (name)

F, f

Old Icelandic	English
fá	get
faðir	father
færði	took
fætur	feet
fagra	fair
fagri	fair
fái	get
fáir	few
fallinn	fallen
fallnir	fallen
fann	found
far	go
fár	unresponsive
fara	go, travel, travelled, travelled, went
farið	travel
farinn	travelling
farmanna	farmers
fastnaði	betrothed
fé	wealth
feðgar	father-and-son
féfátt	money-few
féið	fee
fékk	got, married

Old Icelandic	English
félag	company
félags	company
féll	fell
féllu	fell
fengið	caught
ferð	journey, travel
ferðinni	travelling
féþurfa	fee-needing
fimm	five, give
fimmta	five
finna	found
fjandlega	fiendishly
fjandskapur	fiendship
fjár	wealth
fjárheimtingum	finances
fjárhlut	fee-lot, fee-lots
fjárhluti	possessions
fjárláninu	fee-loaning
fjárláns	fee-loan
fjárlánstillaga	loan-proposal
fjárreiður	finances
fjarri	away
fjárskiptis	fee-exchange
flestum	most
flettir	Fleecer (name)
fljót	river
fljótinu	river
Fljótsdalsheiði	Fljotsdalsheidi (place)
Fljótsdalshéraði	Flotsdal-district (place)
flýti	hurry
flýttu	hurry
föður	father
föðurbróðir	father-brother
fór	travelled, went
fóru	travelled, went
förum	travel, travelling
förunautar	companions
fóstbræður	foster-brothers
fóstra	foster, fosterer
fóstri	fosterer
frá	away, from
frænda	kinsman
frændi	cousin, kinsman
frændur	kinsmen
fram	from

Old Icelandic	English
framan	in-front-of
frásögu	from-saying
frétti	heard
fríðust	most-beautiful
frýði	persuaded
fullkominn	full-coming
fulltingi	assistance
fullur	full
fund	find, to-meet
fundar	meet
fundinn	found
fundust	found
fyrir	before, for
fyrr	before
fyrst	first
fyrstu	first

G, g

Old Icelandic	English
gabbaðir	mocked
gaf	gave
gáfu	gave
gakk	go
gamall	old
gamla	old
gamlan	old
ganga	go, going
gangast	go
gat	got
gaum	heed
gefa	give
gefið	given
gefist	given
gefur	gave
gegnum	through
Geiti	Geiti (name)
Geitir	Geitir (name)
Geitis	Geitis (name)
gekk	going, went
geldur	paid
gengið	gone
gengu	went
gengur	went
gengust	went
ger	made
gera	do, done
gerast	will-be
gerði	did, gave, made
gerðist	became
gerðu	did
gerðust	made
geri	make
gerist	was
gert	done, made
gesti	guests
getið	told-of
gjalda	debt
glöggvastur	sharpest
góðan	good
góðar	good
góðir	good
goðorð	chieftan
góður	good
Göngu-Hrólfssonar	Son-of-Gongu-Hrolf (name)
góss	estate
góssi	belongings
gott	good
græddi	profited
græfu	dig
grályndur	malicious
greiða	assistance
greinilega	clearly
griðkona	the-house-keeper
griðkonuna	house-maiden
griðungarnir	bulls
griðungur	bull
gröf	ditch
gröfina	ditch
gröfinni	the-ditch
Guðrún	Gudrun (name)
gullhöttur	gold-hat
gullreknu	gold-plated

H, h

Old Icelandic	English
hætta	leave
haf	have
hafa	at-sea, had, have
hafði	had

Old Icelandic	English
hafi	had, sea
hag	benefit
Hákonar	Hakon (name)
hald	hold
haldast	held
hálft	half-share
Hallkötlu	Hallkotla (name)
Hálogaland	Halogaland (place)
háls	hills
hálsi	neck
handa	hand
hann	he, him, his
hans	his
harðla	harden
hásetum	crew
haustið	autumn
hávaðamaður	a-loud-man
héðan	from-here
hefði	would-have
hefðu	had
hefi	have
hefir	had, has, have
heillavænlegra	beneficial
heim	home
heima	home
heimagriðunginum	home-bull
heimagriðungurinn	home-bull, home-bulls
heimamaður	home-man
heiman	home
heimtir	demanded
heimtu	demand
heiti	named
heitin	named
heitir	named
heitorði	title
heldur	held, rather
Helga	Helga (name)
Helgi	Helgi (name)
Helgu	Helga (name), Helga's (name)
hélt	held
hendi	hand
hendur	hand, hands
hennar	her
hér	here
héraðið	district

Old Icelandic	English
herbergjum	rooms
herfilegan	harrowing-like
hesta	horses
hét	named, names
hétu	named
hið	the
hin	the
hina	the
hingað	here
hinn	him, the
hins	the
hitt	other
hitta	meet
hitti	met
hittu	met
hjá	beside
hlaðinu	farmyard
hlaupa	jump
hlaut	got
hleypur	ran
hljóp	ran
hlógu	laughed
hlóst	laughed
hlotist	lot
hlut	share
hluti	things
Hnefilsdal	Hnefilsdal (place)
höfði	head
höfðingi	chief
höfðingja	chieftans
höfðu	had
Hofi	Hof (place)
Hofland	Hofland (place)
Hofs	Hof (place)
Hofsmönnum	Men-of-Hof (place)
höfuð	head
höfum	have
Hofverja	of-Hof (place)
hol	hole
hönd	hand
höndina	hand
honum	he, him, his
Hrafnssonar	Son-of-Hrafn (name)
Hrani	Hrani (name)
hrapa	hurried

Old Icelandic	English
Hróðgeirs	Hrodgeir (name)
hross	horses
hrossin	horses
hrumur	decrepit
hug	thought, thoughts
hugar	mind
hugkvæmur	resourceful
hugmannlega	mentally
hugsað	know
hugur	thought
hún	she
húsinu	of-the-house
húskarla	house-carls
húskarlar	house-carls
hvar	where
hvarf	disappeared
hver	who
hvergi	nowhere
hverjir	why
hverju	how
hvern	what
hvert	each
hví	why
hvíta	white
hvíti	white
hvorratveggja	either-side
hvort	either, whether

I, i

Old Icelandic	English
illa	badly, ill
illt	ill
Ingibjörg	Ingibjorg (name)
inn	in, then
inni	in, the

Í, í

Old Icelandic	English
í	about, among, at, his, if, in, of, that, the, to, with
ílentust	landed
Íslandi	Iceland (place)
Íslands	Iceland (place)

J, j

Old Icelandic	English
jafnaðarmaður	equally-man, equal-man
jafnan	equally
jafnræði	equally
jarls	earl
játar	accepts
jöfnum	equal
Jökulsá	Jokulsla (place)

K, k

Old Icelandic	English
kæmi	came
kalla	called
kallaður	called
kallar	calls
karl	man
kaupbrigði	bargains
kaupir	bought
kaus	chose
kemur	came
kenndi	knew
Ketilssonar	Son-of-Ketil (name)
keypti	bought
kippti	snatched
klyfjar	hoof
klyfjum	hooves
kné	knee
koglaði	quivered
kom	came
koma	came, come, comes
komast	come
komið	come, coming
kominn	came, come, coming
komni	coming
komnir	came, coming
komu	came
kona	wife, woman
konan	woman
konu	wife, woman
konuna	wife
kört	short

Old Icelandic	English
Körtur	Kartur (name)
kostur	choice
Kraka	Kraki (name)
Krakadóttur	daughter-of-Kraka (name)
krakalæk	krakalaek
Kraki	Kraki (name)
Krossavík	Krossavik (place)
kumpánar	companions
kunna	knowing
kvað	said
kvaðst	said, spoke
kveða	sang
kveðst	said
kveður	said
kvenna	woman, women
kvikfé	livestock
kvonfang	wife
kvongaður	married

L, l

Old Icelandic	English
lá	laid, lay
laðaði	attracted
Lagarfljót	Lagarfljot (place)
lagði	laid, left
lagðist	lay
lagður	laid
lán	loan
land	land
landi	land
landnámum	land-taking
langlífur	long-life
láta	leave, let
latti	discouraged
launa	repay
legg	lay
leggur	laid
leið	passed, way
leigðu	rented
leitaði	sought
lék	played
lendur	land
lengur	longer
lést	let
lét	had, let
letja	let
létt	let
létu	yet
leystur	loosened
liðfær	team-working
liði	company
liðinu	team
liðnum	passed
lifa	live
lifði	lived
líka	alike
líkast	like
lítið	little
lítil	little
litlu	little
lítt	little
lögðu	laid
lögðust	laid
lokið	ended
lönd	lands
lýkst	ended
lýkur	ends

M, m

Old Icelandic	English
má	may
maður	man
mædd	tired
mælti	said, spoke
mágs	brother-in-law
mágur	brother-in-law
mál	matter, matters
máli	matter, speak, speak
máls	matter
málugur	talkative
mann	men
manna	men, people
mannanar	accomplishment
mannbrodda	man-shaft
mannbroddarnir	spear
mannvænlegasti	man-most-promising
mannvænlegir	men-promising
marga	many
margbreytinn	many-varied

Old Icelandic	English
máttu	could
mátust	discussed
með	with
meðallagi	middle-lying
meðan	long-as, with
meira	more
Melrakkasléttu	Melrakkasletta (place)
menn	men
mér	me, my, to-me
mest	most
mesta	most
mesti	best
meta	appreciate
metnaðar	ambition
Miðfjörð	Midfjord (place)
mig	me
mikið	much
mikil	much
mikill	great, much
mikilli	much
mikilmenni	great-man
mikinn	much
miklu	much
milli	between
millum	between
mín	for-me, mine, my
minn	mine
minni	less
minnkaðist	lessened
mínum	mine
missti	lost
mitt	mine
mjög	much, very
Möðrudalsheiði	Modrudalsheidi (place)
mönnum	men, people
morgun	morning
morguns	morning
mun	shall, will
mundi	would
mundu	should, would, would-be
muntu	shall
munu	shall

N, n

Old Icelandic	English
næsta	next
nætur	nights
nafna	namesake
nafni	namesake
Naumudal	Naumudal (place)
naut	bulls
nautanna	bull
nefndist	named
nefndur	named
neitað	denied
nenni	care
niður	down
nöfn	names
nokkuð	some, somewhat
nokkur	some
nokkura	some
norðarlega	northerly
norður	north
Noreg	Norway (place)
Noregi	Norway (place)
Noregs	Norway (place)
nótt	night
nú	not, now
numin	taken
nýkomin	newly-arrived, newly-come
nýtekið	newly-taken

O, o

Old Icelandic	English
of	of
ofan	above, down, over
ofráð	too-high
ofsamaður	over-bearing-man
og	also, and
okkar	ours
orð	word
orðsending	message
orðstír	reputation
orðum	words
Ormsár	Ormsa (place)
oss	us

Old Icelandic	English

Ó, ó

Old Icelandic	English
ódæll	unruly
ófriði	war
ógurlegur	formidable
ólíklegur	unlikely
Ósk	Osk (name)
Ósvaldsson	Son-of-Osvald (name)
óvæginn	ruthless
óvinveitts	unfriendly
óvís	uncertain
óx	grew

Ö, ö

Old Icelandic	English
öðrum	other
öll	all
öllu	all
öllum	all
Ölvir	Olvir (name)
Önundur	Onund (name)
Öxarfirði	Oxarfjord (place)
Öxna-Þórissonar	Son-of-Oxna-Thori (name)

R, r

Old Icelandic	English
ráð	advice
ráðabreytni	decision-conduct
ráðahag	proposed
ráðahagsins	consult
ráði	advice
ráðir	advise
ráðist	advise
ráðs	advice
ráðum	advice
ræðir	discussed
ræðst	decided
rammur	strong
rannsaka	search
réð	advised
reið	rode
reisir	raised
rekaströndum	rekastrondum
rekkjunnar	bed
Reyðarfjörð	Reydarfjord (place)
reyndist	turned-out
ríða	ride, rode
riðið	rode
ríður	rode
risinn	risen
röskur	strong
röskvasti	most-mature
rufu	tore
rúmi	room

S, s

Old Icelandic	English
sá	saw, so, the
sækir	fetched
sækja	seek
sæmst	same
sætt	settlement
sagði	said, said, told, told
sagðist	said
sagt	said, said
sakagiftir	sake-given
sakar	sake, sake-of
saman	together
samfarar	interaction
sanna	truth
sannlegt	true-like
satt	truth
sauðhús	sheep-house
segði	said
segi	said
segir	said, say, told
segist	said
segja	say, tell, to-say
seinkaði	delayed
sekur	guilty
sel	sell
seldi	sold
seldurunum	from-the-hut-door
selið	shed
selinu	shed
sels	shed

Old Icelandic	English
selt	sold
selvegginum	shed-ways
sem	as, was, which
sér	as, he, him, himself, his, saw, that, themselves, this, with
sérlega	especially
setja	sit
sett	set
síðan	after, afterwards, since
síðar	afterwards
síður	less
síðustu	finally
sig	himself
Sigurður	Sigurd (name)
sína	his, theirs
sinn	his, that
sinni	his
síns	his
sínu	his, theirs
sínum	his, theirs
sitt	his
sjálfdæmi	self-example
sjálfur	himself
sjö	seven
sjóði	funds
sjónina	sight
skaði	loss
skálagerðar	hut-make
skalt	shall
skamma	short
skapi	mood
skaplyndi	mind, temper, temperament
skaplyndis	temper
skapraun	temperament
Skeggjastöðum	Skeggjastadir (place)
skemmsta	shortest
skemmu	storehouse
skemmuna	sleeping-room
skikkju	cloak
skildu	separated
skildumst	parted
skiljast	separated
skip	ship, ships

Old Icelandic	English
skipi	ship
skipið	ship
skipmenn	ship-men
skips	ship, ships
skipsöluna	ship's-sale
skipta	divided
skipti	changed
skjöldinn	shield
skjótt	quickly, soon
skóg	forest
skóm	shoes
skuld	should
skuldalið	indebted
skuldastaðurinn	debt
skuldunauturinn	debtor
skuluð	should
skyldi	should, would
skyldu	should, would
skylt	should
skyrbjúg	scurvy
slá	struck
slíkt	such
Smjörvatnsheiði	Smjorvatnsheidi (place)
snarar	sneaked
snemma	early
sneri	turned
sneypu	shame
sögu	saga
sögunni	the-saga
sömu	same
son	son
sonar	son, son's
sonu	sons
sonur	son, son-of
sótt	sickness
sóttir	sought
sóttu	sought
spjót	spear
spjóti	spear
spjótið	spear
spjótinu	spear
spottar	mocked
sprettur	sprang
spurði	asked
spurður	asked

Old Icelandic	English
spurðust	learned-of
stað	place
staðar	place
staddur	standing
standa	stand
stangar	stabbed
stangast	stabbed
Steinbirni	Steinbjorn (name)
Steinbjarnar	Steinbjorn (name), Steinbjorn's (name)
Steinbjörn	Steinbjorn (name)
sterkur	strong
stóð	stood
stoða	stood
stöðli	standing
stökk	fled
stönguðust	stabbing
stór	great, large
stóra	great
stórmannlegur	great-man-like
stund	awhile, while
stundar	awhile
sumar	summer
sumarið	summer
sumri	summer
sumur	summers
svaraði	answered
svarar	answered
svefns	sleep
svefnskemmunnar	sleeping-room
sveinninn	boy
Sveinungsvík	Sveinungsvik (place)
sveitarhöfðingi	rural-chief
svívirti	dishonoured
svo	so
svör	answer
synir	sons
synja	refuse

T, t

Old Icelandic	English
tæki	take
taka	take, took
takast	take
tekur	take, took
telur	counted
tíðinda	news
tíðindi	news, tidings
tíðindin	news
tíðindum	news
til	for, to, until
tillags	proposal
tilsögu	to-say
tímum	time
Tóftavelli	Toftavellir (place)
tók	took
tókust	took
trúa	trusted
trúið	trust
tuttugu	twenty
tveir	two
tvo	two
tvö	two

Þ, þ

Old Icelandic	English
þá	then
það	it, that, the
þaðan	from-there
þangað	from-there
þann	he, that
þar	then, there
þau	the, then, they
þegar	already, straight-away, then, when
þeim	that, the, them, they
þeir	they
þeirra	of-them, their, theirs, they
þeirrar	their, there
þér	to-you, you, your
þess	this
þessa	this
þessari	this
þessu	this
þetta	that, the, this
Þiðranda	Thidrandi (name)
þig	you
þiggja	accept, receive
þín	you

Old Icelandic	English
þinn	yours
þinni	yours
þíns	yours
þínum	your, yours
Þistilsfjarðar	Thistilsfjord (place)
þitt	yours
þó	though
Þóra	Thora (name)
Þorbjarnar	Thorbjorn (name), Thorbjorn's (name)
Þorbjörg	Thorbjorg (name)
Þorbjörn	Thorbjorn (name)
Þórður	Thord (name)
Þorfinns	Thorfin's (name)
Þorfinnsson	Son-of-Thorfin (name)
Þorfinnssyni	son-of-Thorfin (name)
Þorfinnur	Thorfin (name)
Þorgerður	Thorgerd (name)
Þorgils	Thorgils (name)
Þorgilsi	Thorgils's (name)
Þorgilsson	Son-of-Thorgils (name)
Þóri	Thori (name)
Þórir	Thori (name)
Þóris	Thorir (name)
Þórisdóttur	Daughter-of-Thorri (name)
Þórisson	Son-of-Thorri (name)
Þorkell	Thorkell (name)
Þorstein	Thorstein (name)
Þorsteini	Thorstein (name)
Þorsteinn	Thorstein (name)
Þorsteins	Thorstein (name), Thorstein's (name)
Þorsteinsson	Son-of-Thorstein (name)
þorum	dare
þótti	seemed, thought, thought-of
þóttist	thought
þrevetur	three-winters
þriðji	third
þrítugur	thirty
þrjá	three
þryms	thrymr
þú	you
þungt	unhappy
þurfa	needed
þurfti	needed
því	because, for, since, that, then, therefore
þykir	considered, seemed, think
þykist	seemed
þykja	thought

U, u

Old Icelandic	English
ullhött	woolen-hat
um	about
umsýslu	administered, administration, administrations
undan	away, away-from, under
unga	young
uns	until
upp	up
upphafsmaður	instigator
uppi	up
urðu	became
utan	out, out-of
utanferðar	out-travel
uxu	grow

Ú, ú

Old Icelandic	English
úr	from, out-from, out-of
út	back, back-from, out
úti	about, outside

V, v

Old Icelandic	English
vænn	kind
vænst	fair
væri	was, would-be
væru	were
vakti	awoke
vanda	problems
vanfær	disabled
vanhluta	part

Old Icelandic	English
var	was
varð	became, was
vaskasti	boldest
vasklegur	diligent
vatn	water
veg	way
vegginum	roof
veit	know
veitti	grant
vek	wake
vekja	awoke
vel	well
ver	be
vér	we
vera	be, been, had-been
verða	be, become
verði	be
verður	became, bring
verið	be, became, been, made
versna	worst
vestur	west
Vesturdalsár	Vesturdalsa (place)
vesuðust	felt
vetra	winters
vetrum	winters
vetur	winter, winters
veturhúsum	winter-house
veturinn	winter
við	therefore, with
viðum	wood
viðurnefni	nickname
víg	killing
vil	will, wish
vildi	will, willed, wished
vilja	will, willed
viljum	will
vill	will
vilt	will
viltu	will-you
vinátta	friendship
vináttu	friendship
vinsælastur	popular
vinsæll	popularity
vinsælust	popular
vinur	friend

Old Icelandic	English
vinveittur	friendly
virðingar	worthiness
virðist	seems
virður	respect
virti	valued
víss	sure, surely
vissi	knew
víst	certainly
vita	knew, know
vitað	know
viturlega	wise-like
vonbiðill	hopeful
Vopnafirði	Vopnafjord (place)
Vopnafjarðar	Vopnafjord (place)
Vopnafjarðarár	Vopnafjord (place)
Vopnafjörð	Vopnafjord (place)
Vopnfirðinga	Vopnafjord (place)
vor	spring
vörðust	guarded
vorið	spring
voru	ours, was, were
vöru	wares
vottar	witnesses

Y, y

Old Icelandic	English
yfir	across, over
yrði	would
Yrjar	Yrjar (place)

Word List *(English to Old Icelandic)*

English	Old Icelandic

A, a

English	Old Icelandic
a	*að*
about	*á, áður, í, um, úti*
above	*ofan*
accept	*þiggja*
accepts	*játar*
accomplishment	*mannanar*
across	*yfir*
action	*bregðir*
administered	*umsýslu*
administration	*umsýslu*
administrations	*umsýslu*
advice	*ráð, ráði, ráðs, ráðum*
advise	*ráðir, ráðist*
advised	*réð*
after	*eftir, síðan*
afterwards	*síðan, síðar*
again	*aftur*
age	*aldri*
alike	*líka*
all	*alla, allan, allir, allra, allri, alls, allt, öll, öllu, öllum*
all-little-quiet	*alllítilþægur*
alone	*ein, einn, eitt*
a-loud-man	*hávaðamaður*
already	*þegar*
also	*og*
am	*á, em*
ambition	*metnaðar*
among	*í*
and	*á, en, og*
another	*annar, annars*
answer	*svör*
answered	*svaraði, svarar*
anything-else	*annað*
appreciate	*meta*
are	*á, ert, eru*
are-you	*ertu*
as	*á, að, er, sem, sér*
ask	*bið, biðja*
asked	*bað, beiddist, beiðist, biðji, biður, spurði, spurður*
assistance	*fulltingi, greiða*
Asvar (name)	*Ásvarar*
asvar's	*ásvarar*
Asvor (name)	*Ásvör*
at	*á, að, í*
Atlavik (place)	*Atlavík*
Atli (name)	*Atla*
at-sea	*hafa*
attracted	*laðaði*
autumn	*haustið*
away	*brott, brottu, fjarri, frá, undan*
away-from	*undan*
awhile	*stund, stundar*
awoke	*vakti, vekja*

B, b

English	Old Icelandic
back	*aftur, bak, út*
back-from	*út*
badly	*illa*
bargains	*kaupbrigði*
be	*er, ver, vera, verða, verði, verið*
bear	*bera*
became	*gerðist, urðu, varð, verður, verið*
because	*því*
become	*verða*
bed	*rekkjunnar*
been	*vera, verið*
before	*áður, fyrir, fyrr*
behind	*eftir*
believed	*átrúnaður*
belongings	*góssi*
beneficial	*heillavænlegra*
benefit	*hag*
beside	*hjá*
best	*best, bestur, mesti*
betrothed	*fastnaði*

English	Old Icelandic
between	*milli, millum*
bid	*bað, báðu, biður, bjóða*
blind	*blindan*
boldest	*vaskasti*
Bolungarhof (place)	*Bulungarhöfn*
Bolungarvollu (place)	*Bulungarvöllu*
born	*barna*
borne	*borið*
both	*báðir, bæði*
bought	*kaupir, keypti*
bound	*bundu*
boy	*sveinninn*
bridge	*brú*
bring	*verður*
Brodd-Helgi (name)	*Brodd-Helga, Brodd-Helgi*
brother-in-law	*mágs, mágur*
brothers	*bræðra, bræðrum, bræður*
Brynolf's (name)	*Brynjólfs*
bull	*griðungur, nautanna*
bulls	*griðungarnir, naut*
but	*en*
by	*á*

C, c

English	Old Icelandic
called	*kalla, kallaður*
calls	*kallar*
came	*kæmi, kemur, kom, koma, kominn, komnir, komu*
care	*nenni*
carried	*borinn*
caught	*fengið*
certainly	*víst*
changed	*breytti, skipti*
chief	*höfðingi*
chieftan	*goðorð*
chieftans	*höfðingja*
childhood	*barnæsku*
children	*barna, börn*
choice	*kostur*
chose	*kaus*
clearly	*greinilega*
cloak	*skikkju*
come	*koma, komast, komið, kominn*
comes	*koma*
coming	*komið, kominn, komni, komnir*
companions	*förunautar, kumpánar*
company	*félag, félags, liði*
compensate	*bæta, bætir*
considerable	*ærið*
considered	*þykir*
consult	*ráðahagsins*
could	*máttu*
counted	*telur*
cousin	*frændi*
crew	*hásetum*

D, d

English	Old Icelandic
dare	*þorum*
daughter	*dóttir, dóttur*
daughter-of-Kraka (name)	*Krakadóttur*
Daughter-of-Thorri (name)	*Þórisdóttur*
daughters	*dætur*
day	*dag*
dead	*dauðan, dauður*
death	*andlát, dauða, dauðs, daun*
debt	*gjalda, skuldastaðurinn*
debtor	*skuldunauturinn*
decided	*ræðst*
decision-conduct	*ráðabreytni*
decrepit	*hrumur*
deep	*djúpa*
delayed	*seinkaði*
demand	*heimtu*
demanded	*heimtir*
denied	*neitað*
did	*gerði, gerðu*
died	*andaðist, dó*
dig	*græfu*
diligent	*vasklegur*

English	Old Icelandic
disabled	*vanfær*
disappeared	*hvarf*
discouraged	*latti*
discussed	*mátust, ræðir*
dishonoured	*svívirti*
district	*héraðið*
ditch	*gröf, gröfina*
divided	*skipta*
do	*gera*
done	*gera, gert*
door	*durunum*
down	*niður, ofan*
dwelling	*búið*
dwelt	*bjó*

E, e

English	Old Icelandic
each	*hvert*
earl	*jarls*
early	*snemma*
ears	*eyru*
easily-seen	*auðséð*
east	*austan, austur*
eastern-man	*austmanni*
eastern-men	*austmenn, austmönnum*
eight	*átta*
eighteen	*átján*
Einar (name)	*Einar, Einari*
Einar's (name)	*Einars*
either	*hvort*
either-side	*hvorratveggja*
ended	*lokið, lýkst*
ends	*lýkur*
equal	*jöfnum*
equally	*jafnan, jafnræði*
equally-man	*jafnaðarmaður*
equal-man	*jafnaðarmaður*
especially	*sérlega*
estate	*bú, búi, búinu, góss*
eye-injury	*augnaverk*
Eyvind (name)	*Eyvindur*

F, f

English	Old Icelandic
fair	*fagra, fagri, vænst*
fair-wind	*byr*
fallen	*fallinn, fallnir*
farm	*bæ, búsins*
farm-bulls	*búigriðunginum*
farmers	*farmanna*
farmyard	*hlaðinu*
father	*faðir, föður*
father-and-son	*feðgar*
father-brother	*föðurbróðir*
fee	*féið*
fee-exchange	*fjárskiptis*
fee-loan	*fjárláns*
fee-loaning	*fjárláninu*
fee-lot	*fjárhlut*
fee-lots	*fjárhlut*
fee-needing	*féþurfa*
feet	*fætur*
fell	*féll, féllu*
fellow	*drengur*
fellow-like	*drengilega*
felt	*vesuðust*
fetched	*sækir*
few	*fáir*
fiendishly	*fjandlega*
fiendship	*fjandskapur*
finally	*síðustu*
finances	*fjárheimtingum, fjárreiður*
find	*fund*
first	*fyrst, fyrstu*
five	*fimm, fimmta*
fled	*stökk*
Fleecer (name)	*flettir*
Fljotsdalsheidi (place)	*Fljótsdalsheiði*
Flotsdal-district (place)	*Fljótsdalshéraði*
for	*að, fyrir, því, til*
force	*afli*
forest	*skóg*
for-me	*mín*
formidable	*ógurlegur*
foster	*fóstra*
foster-brothers	*fóstbræður*
fosterer	*fóstra, fóstri*

English	Old Icelandic
found	*fann, finna, fundinn, fundust*
friend	*vinur*
friendly	*vinveittur*
friendship	*vinátta, vináttu*
from	*af, frá, fram, úr*
from-here	*héðan*
from-saying	*frásögu*
from-the-hut-door	*seldurunum*
from-there	*þaðan, þangað*
full	*fullur*
full-coming	*fullkominn*
funds	*sjóði*

G, g

English	Old Icelandic
gave	*gaf, gáfu, gefur, gerði*
Geiti (name)	*Geiti*
Geitir (name)	*Geitir*
Geitis (name)	*Geitis*
get	*fá, fái*
give	*fimm, gefa*
given	*gefið, gefist*
go	*far, fara, gakk, ganga, gangast*
going	*ganga, gekk*
gold-hat	*gullhöttur*
gold-plated	*gullreknu*
gone	*gengið*
good	*góðan, góðar, góðir, góður, gott*
got	*fékk, gat, hlaut*
grandfather	*afa*
grant	*veitti*
great	*mikill, stór, stóra*
great-man	*mikilmenni*
great-man-like	*stórmannlegur*
grew	*óx*
grow	*uxu*
guarded	*vörðust*
Gudrun (name)	*Guðrún*
guests	*gesti*
guilty	*sekur*

H, h

English	Old Icelandic
had	*ætti, átti, áttu, hafa, hafði, hafi, hefðu, hefir, höfðu, lét*
had-been	*vera*
Hakon (name)	*Hákonar*
half-share	*hálft*
Hallkotla (name)	*Hallkötlu*
Halogaland (place)	*Hálogaland*
hand	*handa, hendi, hendur, hönd, höndina*
hands	*hendur*
harden	*harðla*
harrowing-like	*herfilegan*
has	*hefir*
have	*haf, hafa, hefi, hefir, höfum*
he	*á, hann, honum, sér, þann*
head	*ennið, höfði, höfuð*
heard	*frétti*
heed	*gaum*
held	*haldast, heldur, hélt*
Helga (name)	*Helga, Helgu*
Helga's (name)	*Helgu*
Helgi (name)	*Helgi*
her	*hennar*
here	*hér, hingað*
hills	*háls*
him	*hann, hinn, honum, sér*
himself	*sér, sig, sjálfur*
his	*hann, hans, honum, í, sér, sína, sinn, sinni, síns, sínu, sínum, sitt*
Hnefilsdal (place)	*Hnefilsdal*
Hof (place)	*Hofi, Hofs*
Hofland (place)	*Hofland*
hold	*hald*
hole	*hol*
home	*heim, heima, heiman*
home-bull	*heimagriðunginum, heimagriðungurinn*
home-bulls	*heimagriðungurinn*
home-man	*heimamaður*

English	Old Icelandic
hoof	*klyfjar*
hooves	*klyfjum*
hopeful	*vonbiðill*
horses	*hesta, hross, hrossin*
house-carls	*húskarla, húskarlar*
house-maiden	*griðkonuna*
how	*hverju*
Hrani (name)	*Hrani*
Hrodgeir (name)	*Hróðgeirs*
hurried	*hrapa*
hurry	*flýti, flýttu*
hut-make	*skálagerðar*

I, i

English	Old Icelandic
i	*eg*
Iceland (place)	*Íslandi, Íslands*
if	*ef, er, í*
ill	*illa, illt*
improved	*batnaði*
in	*á, í, inn, inni*
indebted	*skuldalið*
in-front-of	*framan*
Ingibjorg (name)	*Ingibjörg*
inheritance	*arfs*
instigator	*upphafsmaður*
intended	*ætla, ætlaði, ætluðu*
interaction	*samfarar*
into	*á*
invitation	*boðið*
invited	*bauð*
is	*er*
it	*á, það*

J, j

English	Old Icelandic
Jokulsla (place)	*Jökulsá*
journey	*ferð*
jump	*hlaupa*

K, k

English	Old Icelandic
Kartur (name)	*Körtur*
killed	*drápu, drepinn*
killing	*víg*
kill-we	*drepum*
kind	*vænn*
kinsman	*frænda, frændi*
kinsmen	*frændur*
knee	*kné*
knew	*kenndi, vissi, vita*
know	*hugsað, veit, vita, vitað*
knowing	*kunna*
krakalaek	*krakalæk*
Kraki (name)	*Kraka, Kraki*
Krossavik (place)	*Krossavík*

L, l

English	Old Icelandic
Lagarfljot (place)	*Lagarfljót*
laid	*lá, lagði, lagður, leggur, lögðu, lögðust*
land	*land, landi, lendur*
landed	*ílentust*
lands	*lönd*
land-taking	*landnámum*
large	*stór*
laughed	*hlógu, hlóst*
lay	*lá, lagðist, legg*
learned-of	*spurðust*
leave	*hætta, láta*
left	*lagði*
less	*minni, síður*
lessened	*minnkaðist*
let	*láta, lést, lét, letja, létt*
like	*líkast*
little	*lítið, lítil, litlu, lítt*
live	*lifa*
lived	*bjó, búið, lifði*
livestock	*kvikfé*
loan	*lán*
loan-proposal	*fjárlánstillaga*
long-as	*meðan*
longer	*lengur*
long-life	*langlífur*
loosened	*leystur*
loss	*skaði*

English	*Old Icelandic*
lost	*missti*
lot	*hlotist*
love	*ástir*

M, m

English	*Old Icelandic*
made	*ger, gerði, gerðust, gert, verið*
make	*geri*
malicious	*grályndur*
man	*karl, maður*
man-most-promising	*mannvænlegasti*
man-shaft	*mannbrodda*
many	*marga*
many-varied	*margbreytinn*
marriage-proposal	*bónorðið*
married	*átti, fékk, kvongaður*
matter	*mál, máli, máls*
matters	*mál*
may	*má*
me	*mér, mig*
meet	*fundar, hitta*
Melrakkasletta (place)	*Melrakkasléttu*
men	*mann, manna, menn, mönnum*
Men-of-Hof (place)	*Hofsmönnum*
men-promising	*mannvænlegir*
mentally	*hugmannlega*
message	*orðsending*
met	*hitti, hittu*
method	*aðferð*
middle-lying	*meðallagi*
Midfjord (place)	*Miðfjörð*
mind	*hugar, skaplyndi*
mine	*eg, mín, minn, mínum, mitt*
mocked	*gabbaðir, spottar*
Modrudalsheidi (place)	*Möðrudalsheiði*
money-few	*féfátt*
mood	*skapi*
more	*meira*
morning	*morgun, morguns*
most	*flestum, mest, mesta*
most-beautiful	*fríðust*
most-mature	*röskvasti*
much	*mikið, mikil, mikill, mikilli, mikinn, miklu, mjög*
my	*mér, mín*

N, n

English	*Old Icelandic*
named	*heiti, heitin, heitir, hét, hétu, nefndist, nefndur*
names	*hét, nöfn*
namesake	*nafna, nafni*
Naumudal (place)	*Naumudal*
neck	*hálsi*
needed	*þurfa, þurfti*
newly-arrived	*nýkomin*
newly-come	*nýkomin*
newly-taken	*nýtekið*
news	*tíðinda, tíðindi, tíðindin, tíðindum*
next	*annan, næsta*
nickname	*viðurnefni*
night	*nótt*
nights	*nætur*
no	*eigi*
noble	*ættar*
none	*eigi, engan, engi*
no-one	*engi*
north	*norður*
northerly	*norðarlega*
Norway (place)	*Noreg, Noregi, Noregs*
not	*eigi, einskis, ekki, nú*
now	*nú*
nowhere	*hvergi*

O, o

English	*Old Icelandic*
of	*á, að, af, í, of*
of-answer	*afsvör*
off	*af*
offered	*bauð*
of-hand	*afhenda*
of-Hof (place)	*Hofverja*

English	Old Icelandic
of-the-house	*húsinu*
of-them	*þeirra*
of-told	*aftaldi*
old	*gamall, gamla, gamlan*
Olvir (name)	*Ölvir*
on	*á*
one	*eina, einn, eitt, enn*
Onund (name)	*Önundur*
Ormsa (place)	*Ormsár*
Osk (name)	*Ósk*
other	*annað, hitt, öðrum*
others	*aðrir*
ours	*okkar, voru*
out	*út, utan*
out-from	*úr*
out-of	*úr, utan*
outside	*úti*
out-travel	*utanferðar*
over	*ofan, yfir*
over-bearing-man	*ofsamaður*
own	*eigið*
owned	*eiga*
Oxarfjord (place)	*Öxarfirði*

P, p

English	Old Icelandic
paid	*geldur*
part	*vanhluta*
parted	*skildumst*
passed	*leið, liðnum*
people	*manna, mönnum*
persuaded	*frýði*
place	*stað, staðar*
played	*lék*
popular	*vinsælastur, vinsælust*
popularity	*vinsæll*
possessions	*fjárhluti*
precious	*dýrri*
prepared	*bjó, búin, búinn, búnir*
problems	*vanda*
profited	*græddi*
promising	*efnilegur*
proposal	*bónorð, tillags*
proposed	*ráðahag*
proposed-to	*bað*

Q, q

English	Old Icelandic
quick	*bráðger*
quickly	*skjótt*
quivered	*koglaði*

R, r

English	Old Icelandic
raised	*reisir*
ran	*hleypur, hljóp*
rather	*heldur*
receive	*þiggja*
refuse	*synja*
rekastrondum	*rekaströndum*
rented	*leigðu*
repay	*launa*
reputation	*orðstír*
resourceful	*hugkvæmur*
respect	*virður*
return	*aftur*
Reydarfjord (place)	*Reyðarfjörð*
ride	*ríða*
risen	*risinn*
river	*fljót, fljótinu*
rode	*reið, ríða, riðið, ríður*
roof	*vegginum*
room	*rúmi*
rooms	*herbergjum*
rural-chief	*sveitarhöfðingi*
ruthless	*óvæginn*

S, s

English	Old Icelandic
saga	*sögu*
said	*kvað, kvaðst, kveðst, kveður, mælti, sagði, sagðist, sagt, segði, segi, segir, segist*
sake	*sakar*
sake-given	*sakagiftir*

English	Old Icelandic
sake-of	*sakar*
same	*sæmst, sömu*
sang	*kveða*
saw	*sá, sér*
say	*segir, segja*
scurvy	*skyrbjúg*
sea	*hafi*
search	*rannsaka*
seek	*sækja*
seemed	*þótti, þykir, þykist*
seems	*virðist*
self-example	*sjálfdæmi*
sell	*sel*
separated	*skildu, skiljast*
set	*sett*
settlement	*sætt*
settlements	*byggðum*
seven	*sjö*
shall	*mun, muntu, munu, skalt*
shame	*sneypu*
share	*hlut*
sharpest	*glöggvastur*
she	*hún*
shed	*selið, selinu, sels*
shed-ways	*selvegginum*
sheep-house	*sauðhús*
shield	*skjöldinn*
ship	*skip, skipi, skipið, skips*
ship-men	*skipmenn*
ships	*skip, skips*
ship's-sale	*skipsöluna*
shoes	*skóm*
short	*kört, skamma*
shortest	*skemmsta*
should	*mundu, skuld, skuluð, skyldi, skyldu, skylt*
sickness	*sótt*
sight	*sjónina*
Sigurd (name)	*Sigurður*
since	*síðan, því*
sit	*setja*
Skeggjastadir (place)	*Skeggjastöðum*
sleep	*svefns*

English	Old Icelandic
sleeping-room	*skemmuna, svefnskemmunnar*
slope	*brekkuna*
Smjorvatnsheidi (place)	*Smjörvatnsheiði*
snatched	*kippti*
sneaked	*snarar*
so	*sá, svo*
sold	*seldi, selt*
some	*nokkuð, nokkur, nokkura*
somewhat	*nokkuð*
son	*son, sonar, sonur*
son-of	*sonur*
Son-of-Gongu-Hrolf (name)	*Göngu-Hrólfssonar*
Son-of-Hrafn (name)	*Hrafnssonar*
Son-of-Ketil (name)	*Ketilssonar*
Son-of-Osvald (name)	*Ósvaldsson*
Son-of-Oxna-Thori (name)	*Öxna-Þórissonar*
Son-of-Thorfin (name)	*Þorfinnsson, Þorfinnssyni*
Son-of-Thorgils (name)	*Þorgilsson*
Son-of-Thorri (name)	*Þórisson*
Son-of-Thorstein (name)	*Þorsteinsson*
sons	*sonu, synir*
son's	*sonar*
soon	*skjótt*
sought	*leitaði, sóttir, sóttu*
speak	*máli*
spear	*mannbroddarnir, spjót, spjóti, spjótið, spjótinu*
spending	*eyðist*
spending-man	*eyðslumaður*
spoke	*kvaðst, mælti*
sprang	*sprettur*
spring	*vor, vorið*
stabbed	*stangar, stangast*
stabbing	*stönguðust*
stand	*standa*
standing	*staddur, stöðli*
startled	*brá*

English	Old Icelandic
Steinbjorn (name)	*Steinbirni, Steinbjarnar, Steinbjörn*
Steinbjorn's (name)	*Steinbjarnar*
stood	*stóð, stoða*
storehouse	*skemmu*
straight-away	*þegar*
strong	*rammur, röskur, sterkur*
struck	*slá*
such	*slíkt*
summer	*sumar, sumarið, sumri*
summers	*sumur*
suppose	*ætla*
sure	*víss*
surely	*víss*
Sveinungsvik (place)	*Sveinungsvík*

T, t

English	Old Icelandic
take	*tæki, taka, takast, tekur*
taken	*numin*
talkative	*málugur*
team	*liðinu*
team-working	*liðfær*
tell	*segja*
temper	*skaplyndi, skaplyndis*
temperament	*skaplyndi, skapraun*
than	*en*
that	*á, að, er, í, sér, sinn, það, þann, þeim, þetta, því*
the	*að, hið, hin, hina, hinn, hins, í, inni, sá, það, þau, þeim, þetta*
the-ditch	*gröfinni*
the-door	*duranna, durunum*
the-house-keeper	*griðkona*
their	*þeirra, þeirrar*
theirs	*sína, sínu, sínum, þeirra*
them	*þeim*
themselves	*sér*
then	*inn, þá, þar, þau, þegar, því*

English	Old Icelandic
there	*þar, þeirrar*
therefore	*því, við*
the-saga	*sögunni*
they	*þau, þeim, þeir, þeirra*
Thidrandi (name)	*Þiðranda*
things	*hluti*
think	*þykir*
third	*þriðji*
thirty	*þrítugur*
this	*sér, þess, þessa, þessari, þessu, þetta*
Thistilsfjord (place)	*Þistilsfjarðar*
Thora (name)	*Þóra*
Thorbjorg (name)	*Þorbjörg*
Thorbjorn (name)	*Þorbjarnar, Þorbjörn*
Thorbjorn's (name)	*Þorbjarnar*
Thord (name)	*Þórður*
Thorfin (name)	*Þorfinnur*
Thorfin's (name)	*Þorfinns*
Thorgerd (name)	*Þorgerður*
Thorgils (name)	*Þorgils*
Thorgils's (name)	*Þorgilsi*
Thori (name)	*Þóri, Þórir*
Thorir (name)	*Þóris*
Thorkell (name)	*Þorkell*
Thorstein (name)	*Þorstein, Þorsteini, Þorsteinn, Þorsteins*
Thorstein's (name)	*Þorsteins*
though	*þó*
thought	*hug, hugur, þótti, þóttist, þykja*
thought-of	*þótti*
thoughts	*hug*
three	*þrjá*
three-winters	*þrevetur*
through	*gegnum*
thrymr	*þryms*
tidings	*tíðindi*
tied	*bindur*
time	*tímum*
time-of-day-meal	*dagverð*
tired	*mædd*
title	*heitorði*
to	*á, að, í, til*
to-ask	*beiddist*
Toftavellir (place)	*Tóftavelli*

English	Old Icelandic
together	*saman*
told	*sagði, segir*
told-of	*getið*
to-me	*mér*
to-meet	*fund*
too-high	*ofráð*
took	*færði, taka, tekur, tók, tókust*
tore	*rufu*
to-say	*segja, tilsögu*
to-you	*þér*
travel	*fara, farið, ferð, förum*
travelled	*fara, fór, fóru*
travelling	*farinn, ferðinni, förum*
trick	*bellibragð*
true-like	*sannlegt*
trust	*trúið*
trusted	*trúa*
truth	*sanna, satt*
turned	*sneri*
turned-out	*reyndist*
twenty	*tuttugu*
two	*tveir, tvo, tvö*

U, u

English	Old Icelandic
uncertain	*óvís*
under	*undan*
unfriendly	*óvinveitts*
unhappy	*þungt*
unlikely	*ólíklegur*
unresponsive	*fár*
unruly	*ódæll*
until	*til, uns*
up	*upp, uppi*
urged	*eggjaði*
us	*oss*

V, v

English	Old Icelandic
valued	*virti*
very	*mjög*
Vesturdalsa (place)	*Vesturdalsár*
Vopnafjord (place)	*Vopnafirði, Vopnafjarðar, Vopnafjarðarár, Vopnafjörð, Vopnfirðinga*

W, w

English	Old Icelandic
wait	*bíða*
wake	*vek*
war	*ófriði*
wares	*vöru*
was	*er, gerist, sem, væri, var, varð, voru*
water	*vatn*
way	*leið, veg*
we	*vér*
wealth	*fé, fjár*
wealthy	*auðigur*
wedding	*brúðkaup, brúðkaupið*
well	*vel*
went	*fara, fór, fóru, gekk, gengu, gengur, gengust*
were	*eru, væru, voru*
west	*vestur*
what	*hvern*
when	*er, þegar*
where	*hvar*
whether	*hvort*
which	*er, sem*
while	*stund*
white	*hvíta, hvíti*
who	*er, hver*
why	*hverjir, hví*
wife	*kona, konu, konuna, kvonfang*
will	*mun, vil, vildi, vilja, viljum, vill, vilt*
will-be	*gerast*
willed	*vildi, vilja*
will-you	*viltu*
winter	*vetur, veturinn*
winter-house	*veturhúsum*
winters	*vetra, vetrum, vetur*
wise-like	*viturlega*

English	*Old Icelandic*
wish	*vil*
wished	*vildi*
with	*í, með, meðan, sér, við*
witnesses	*vottar*
woman	*kona, konan, konu, kvenna*
women	*kvenna*
wood	*viðum*
woolen-hat	*ullhött*
word	*orð*
words	*orðum*
worst	*versna*
worthiness	*virðingar*
would	*mundi, mundu, skyldi, skyldu, yrði*
would-be	*mundu, væri*
would-have	*hefði*

Y, y

yet	*létu*
you	*þér, þig, þín, þú*
young	*unga*
your	*þér, þínum*
yours	*þinn, þinni, þíns, þínum, þitt*
Yrjar (place)	*Yrjar*

A Word Comparison of Old Norse and Old Icelandic Words

Old Norse	Old Icelandic	English
áðr	áður	about
áðr	áður	before
ætta	ætti	had
af	að	of
aftalði	aftaldi	of-told
alllítilþægr	alllítilþægur	all-little-quiet
annarr	annar	another
annat	annað	anything-else
annat	annað	other
aptr	aftur	again
aptr	aftur	back
aptr	aftur	return
Ásvaldsson	Ósvaldsson	Son-of-Osvald (Name)
at	að	as
at	að	at
at	að	that
at	að	to
at	út	back-from
at	út	out
atferð	aðferð	method
Atlavik	Atlavík	Atlavik (Place)
átrúnaðr	átrúnaður	believed
auðigr	auðigur	wealthy
auðsét	auðséð	easily-seen
austr	austur	east
beiddist	beiðist	asked
bezt	best	best
beztr	bestur	best
biði	biðji	asked
biðr	biður	asked
biðr	biður	bid
bindr	bindur	tied
boðit	boðið	invitation
Bolungarhöfn	Bulungarhöfn	Bolungarhof (Place)
Bolungarvöllu	Bulungarvöllu	Bolungarvollu (Place)

Old Norse	Old Icelandic	English
bónorðit	bónorð	proposal
bónorðit	bónorðið	marriage-proposal
borit	borið	borne
bráðgerr	bráðger	quick
bræðr	bræður	brothers
brðr	bræður	brothers
brúðkaup	brúðkaupið	wedding
brúðkaupit	brúðkaupið	wedding
brúñkaupit	brúðkaupið	wedding
bta	bæta	compensate
bú	bæ	farm
búit	búið	dwelling
búit	búið	lived
burt	brott	away
burt	brottu	away
byrr	byr	fair-wind
dætr	dætur	daughters
dauðr	dauður	dead
drengiliga	drengilega	fellow-like
drengr	drengur	fellow
efniligr	efnilegur	promising
einarr	Einar	Einar (Name)
ek	eg	i
ekki	eigi	not
ennit	ennið	head
eptir	eftir	after
eyðslumaðr	eyðslumaður	spending-man
eyvindr	Eyvindur	Eyvind (Name)
fætr	fætur	feet
farit	farið	travel
féit	féið	fee
fekk	fékk	got
fekk	fékk	married
fell	féll	fell
fellu	féllu	fell
fengit	fengið	caught

Old Norse	Old Icelandic	English
féþurfi	féþurfa	fee-needing
fjándliga	fjandlega	fiendishly
fjándskapr	fjandskapur	fiendship
fjár	fjárreiður	finances
fljótsdalshera ði	Fljótsdalshéra ði	Fljotsdalshera di (Place)
flýtti	flýttu	hurry
frændr	frændur	kinsmen
frásögn	frásögu	from-saying
frði	færði	took
friðust	fríðust	most-beautiful
fullr	fullur	full
gefit	gefið	given
gefizt	gefist	given
gefr	gefur	gave
geldr	geldur	paid
gengit	gengið	gone
gengr	gengur	went
getit	getið	told-of
glöggvastr	glöggvastur	sharpest
góðr	góður	good
góz	góss	estate
gózi	góssi	belongings
grafi	græfu	dig
Grályndr	Grályndur	Gralyndr (name)
griðungr	griðungur	bull
gullhöttr	gullhöttur	gold-hat
haustit	haustið	autumn
hávaðamaðr	hávaðamaður	a-loud-man
heðan	héðan	from-here
heillavænligra	heillavænlegr a	beneficial
heimagriðung rinn	heimagriðung urinn	home-bull
heimagriðung rinn	heimagriðung urinn	home-bulls
heimamaðr	heimamaður	home-man
heldr	heldur	rather
helt	hélt	held
hendr	hendur	hand
hendr	hendur	hands
heraðit	héraðið	district
herfiligan	herfilegan	harrowing-like

Old Norse	Old Icelandic	English
hingat	hingað	here
hittir	hitti	met
hlaði	hlaðinu	farmyard
hleypr	hleypur	ran
hlotizt	hlotist	lot
hlótt	hlóst	laughed
hon	hún	she
hrumr	hrumur	decrepit
hugkvæmr	hugkvæmur	resourceful
hugmannliga	hugmannlega	mentally
hugr	hug	thought
hugr	hugur	thought
hugsat	hugsað	know
hvárratveggja	hvorratveggja	either-side
hvárt	hvort	either
hvárt	hvort	whether
hverir	hverjir	why
hverr	hver	who
ílendust	ílentust	landed
in	hin	the
ina	hina	the
inn	hinn	the
ins	hins	the
it	hið	the
jafnaðarmaðr	jafnaðarmaðu r	equally-man
jafnaðarmaðr	jafnaðarmaðu r	equal-man
kallaðr	kallaður	called
kemr	kemur	came
kom	koma	comes
komit	komið	come
komit	komið	coming
kómu	komu	came
körtr	Körtur	Kartur (Name)
kostr	kostur	choice
Krossavik	Krossavík	Krossavik (Place)
kvaðst	kveðst	said
kvánfang	kvonfang	wife
kvángaðr	kvongaður	married
kveðr	kveður	said
lagðr	lagður	laid

Old Norse	Old Icelandic	English	Old Norse	Old Icelandic	English
langlífr	langlífur	long-life	nýtekit	nýtekið	newly-taken
leggr	leggur	laid	ofsamaðr	ofsamaður	over-bearing-man
lendr	lendur	land	ógurligr	ógurlegur	formidable
lengr	lengur	longer	ok	og	and
leystr	leystur	loosened	ólíkligr	ólíklegur	unlikely
lézt	lést	let	Önundr	Önundur	Onund (Name)
liðfárr	liðfær	team-working	or	úr	out-from
lítil	lítið	little	ór	úr	from
lokit	lokið	ended	ór	úr	out-from
maðr	maður	man	ór	úr	out-of
mágr	mágur	brother-in-law	óvíss	óvís	uncertain
málugr	málugur	talkative	óxu	uxu	grow
mannvænligir	mannvænlegir	men-promising	ráðizt	ráðist	advise
mannvænligsti	mannvænlegasti	man-most-promising	ræðr	ræðir	discussed
mdd	mædd	tired	rammr	rammur	strong
mik	mig	me	réðst	ræðst	decided
mikit	mikið	much	riðit	riðið	rode
millum	milli	between	ríðr	ríður	rode
minnkað	minnkaðist	lessened	rit	ærið	considerable
mjök	mjög	much	röskr	röskur	strong
morgins	morguns	morning	sakargiptir	sakagiftir	sake-given
munda	mundi	would	sakir	sakar	sake
myndi	mundi	would	samferðir	samfarar	interaction
myndi	mundu	would	sannligt	sannlegt	true-like
nætr	nætur	nights	sekr	sekur	guilty
nátt	nótt	night	selit	selið	shed
nefndr	nefndur	named	sérliga	sérlega	especially
neitat	neitað	denied	síðr	síður	less
nenna	nenni	care	Sigurðr	Sigurður	Sigurd (Name)
niðr	niður	down	sik	sig	himself
nökk	nokkura	some	sjálfdmi	sjálfdæmi	self-example
nökkur	nokkur	some	sjálfr	sjálfur	himself
nökkura	nokkura	some	sjau	sjö	seven
nökkut	nokkuð	somewhat	skilðim	skildumst	parted
norðarliga	norðarlega	northerly	skipit	skip	ship
norðr	norður	north	skipit	skipið	ship
Nóreg	Noreg	Norway (Place)	skir	sækir	fetched
nóregi	Noregi	Norway (Place)	skja	sækja	seek
Nóregs	Noregs	Norway (Place)	skulda-nautrinn	skuldunauturinn	debtor

Old Norse	Old Icelandic	English
skuldastaðrin n	skuldastaðuri nn	debt
smst	sæmst	same
sonr	sonur	son
sonr	sonur	son-of
spjótit	spjótið	spear
sprettr	sprettur	sprang
spurðr	spurður	asked
staddr	staddur	standing
steinbirni	Steinbjarnar	Steinbjorn's (Name)
sterkr	sterkur	strong
stórmannligr	stórmannlegu r	great-man-like
stórr	stór	great
stórr	stór	large
sumarit	sumarið	summer
svá	svo	so
svaraði	svarar	answered
sviviröi	svívirti	dishonoured
tekr	tekur	take
tekr	tekur	took
þangat	þangað	from-there
þat	það	it
þat	það	that
þeir	þeirra	they
þeira	þeirra	of-them
þeira	þeirra	their
þeira	þeirra	theirs
þeirar	þeirrar	there
þess	þessa	this
þik	þig	you
Þórðr	Þórður	Thord (Name)
Þorfinnr	Þorfinnur	Thorfin (Name)
Þorgerðr	Þorgerður	Thorgerd (Name)
Þorsteinn	Þorstein	Thorstein (Name)
Þorsteins	Þorsteinsson	Son-of-Thorstein (Name)
þóttust	þóttist	thought
þrévetr	þrevetur	three-winters
þriði	þriðji	third
þrítugr	þrítugur	thirty
þurftu	þurfti	needed
þykkir	þykir	considered
þykkir	þykir	seemed
þykkir	þykir	think
þykkist	þykist	seemed
þykkja	þykja	thought
tíðenda	tíðinda	news
tíðendi	tíðindi	news
tíðendi	tíðindi	tidings
tíðendin	tíðindin	news
tíðendum	tíðindum	news
tillag	tillags	proposal
Tóptavelli	Tóftavelli	Toftavellir (Place)
tvá	tvo	two
tvau	tvö	two
unz	uns	until
upphafsmaðr	upphafsmaðu r	instigator
útan	utan	out
útan	utan	out-of
útanferðar	utanferðar	out-travel
væri	væru	were
vánbiðill	vonbiðill	hopeful
vanfærr	vanfær	disabled
vápna	Vopnafjarðar ár	Vopnafjord (Place)
vápnafirði	Vopnafirði	Vopnafjord (Place)
Vápnafjarðar	Vopnafjarðar	Vopnafjord (Place)
vápnafjörð	Vopnafjörð	Vopnafjord (Place)
Vapnfirðinga	Vopnfirðinga	Vopnafjord (Place)
vár	vor	spring
várit	vorið	spring
váru	voru	ours
váru	voru	was
váru	voru	were
vaskligr	vasklegur	diligent
váttar	vottar	witnesses
vera	ver	be
verða	verði	be

Old Norse	Old Icelandic	English
verðr	verður	became
verðr	verður	bring
verit	verið	be
verit	verið	became
verit	verið	been
verit	verið	made
vestr	vestur	west
vestrdalsár	Vesturdalsár	Vesturdalsa (Place)
vetr	vetrum	winters
vetr	vetur	winter
vetr	vetur	winters
vetrhúsum	veturhúsum	winter-house
vetrinn	veturinn	winter
viðrnefni	viðurnefni	nickname
vig	víg	killing
vilda	vildi	will
villt	vilt	will
villtu	viltu	will-you
vinr	vinur	friend
vinsælastr	vinsælastur	popular
vinveittr	vinveittur	friendly
virði	virti	valued
virðr	virður	respect
vit	við	with
vitat	vitað	know
vitrliga	viturlega	wise-like

www.ingramcontent.com/pod-product-compliance
Lightning Source LLC
Chambersburg PA
CBHW051419070526
44584CB00023B/3498

* 9 7 8 1 9 1 8 1 5 7 5 3 6 *